New Directions for
Student Services

John H. Schuh
EDITOR-IN-CHIEF

Elizabeth J. Whitt
ASSOCIATE EDITOR

The Small College Dean

Sarah B. Westfall
EDITOR

Number 116 • Winter 2006
Jossey-Bass
San Francisco

THE SMALL COLLEGE DEAN
Sarah B. Westfall (ed.)
New Directions for Student Services, no. 116
John H. Schuh, Editor-in-Chief
Elizabeth J. Whitt, Associate Editor

NEW DIRECTIONS FOR STUDENT SERVICES (ISSN 0164-7970, e-ISSN 1536-0695) is part of The Jossey-Bass Higher and Adult Education Series and is published quarterly by Wiley Subscription Services, Inc., A Wiley Company, at Jossey-Bass, 989 Market Street, San Francisco, California 94103-1741. Periodicals Postage Paid at San Francisco, California, and at additional mailing offices. POSTMASTER: Send address changes to New Directions for Student Services, Jossey-Bass, 989 Market Street, San Francisco, CA 94103-1741.

New Directions for Student Services is indexed in College Student Personnel Abstracts and Contents Pages in Education.

Microfilm copies of issues and articles are available in 16mm and 35mm, as well as microfiche in 105mm, through University Microfilms Inc., 300 North Zeeb Road, Ann Arbor, Michigan 48106-1346.

SUBSCRIPTIONS cost $80 for individuals and $195 for institutions, agencies, and libraries in the United States. See ordering information page at end of book.

EDITORIAL CORRESPONDENCE should be sent to the Editor-in-Chief, John H. Schuh, N 243 Lagomarcino Hall, Iowa State University, Ames, Iowa 50011.

www.josseybass.com

29.00

CONTENTS

EDITOR'S NOTES

Over the years, many of us who work in small colleges have bemoaned the absence of our institutions and our experiences from the student affairs literature, from preparation program curricula and numerous resources provided by our national associations. Many people of goodwill and limited time (including me) have threatened to sit down and write a book that will begin to fill the considerable gap in the literature. I am glad that the New Directions in Student Services series editors, John Schuh and Elizabeth Whitt, invited me to edit a volume on the small college dean, thereby saving me from following through on my threat. Happily, I was able to convince a handful of bright and insightful colleagues that writing a chapter for this volume was noble and feasible and would be a lot of fun. I will leave it to them to respond to the question of whether writing and contributing their chapters was any of these things. I can only say that I enjoyed every minute of my collaboration with them and hope that they are satisfied with the final volume and their part in it.

This volume and its authors have three important goals. First, we seek to provide a focus on the work of senior student affairs officers in small colleges. Many such people labor well and faithfully in obscurity. We seek to shine a light on the realities of being a dean at a small college. Second, we hope to provide useful information to those who are interested in working in a small college environment. Small colleges are those with 5,000 or fewer students, and we know that the work of deans in these settings differs from the work of deans in larger institutions. Think of this volume as a primer on being a small college dean. We have tried to anticipate the most obvious questions about this work and provide perspectives born of experience. Finally, we hope that this volume may spur more research on the experience of student affairs professionals in small college settings. This volume is not a research report, but our hope is that enterprising researchers will pursue their efforts in the area of small colleges and student affairs work in those settings.

In developing the idea for this volume on the small college dean, I consulted with colleagues about what should be included in it. Joan Claar, former dean of students at DePauw University and Cornell College, and I had developed an outline for a book on small colleges in the mid-1990s. This early collaboration led substantively to the content for this volume. I was not able to persuade her to contribute to this volume, though; retirement and grandchildren are fierce competitors when it comes to asking for time. Even so, her conceptual contributions are worth noting.

NEW DIRECTIONS FOR STUDENT SERVICES, no. 116, Winter 2006 © Wiley Periodicals, Inc.
Published online in Wiley InterScience (www.interscience.wiley.com) • DOI: 10.1002/ss.220

Chapter One charts the territory of both small colleges and the work of the dean. It provides historical context and a current picture of small colleges, their vast diversity, their role in higher education, and the work of the dean. It seeks to answer the question, "Why a volume on the small college dean?"

Chapter Two by Debbie Heida provides a description of the small college dean's portfolio. It addresses the array of functional areas that can fall under the purview of the dean, illustrates how divisions of student affairs can be organized in small colleges, and identifies institutional and societal factors that affect the organization of student affairs work in small colleges.

Douglas Oblander addresses the realities of staffing a small college student affairs division in Chapter Three. He describes the challenges of and provides strategies for recruiting and retaining staff, and provides a helpful perspective on the nature of work in small colleges. His attention to the needs and challenges of early- and mid-career colleagues is especially valuable.

In Chapter Four, Janet Heeter Bass defines the differences between the dean's role and the vice president's role. She provides her own insights, along with those of colleagues at similar institutions, and gives concrete examples of how the work of each role is manifested. Her writing puts the reader in the moment as she navigates both roles.

Bruce Colwell, in Chapter Five on the relationship between academic affairs and student affairs, provides a comprehensive look at the historical, structural, and political factors affecting this essential partnership. He sets out the relevant historical context as well as current and potential models for good collaboration between academic affairs and student affairs on small college campuses.

In the final chapter, William Flanagan carefully considers the future of the small college dean. His long years of experience provide important insights into and specificities in identifying factors that will be most salient for small college deans in the next ten years.

My wish is that one of the fine higher education and student affairs graduate programs that prepare so many new practitioners will develop special expertise in small colleges and attract faculty and graduate students who are interested in doing research in the area. Canisius College offers a college student personnel program that highlights private college settings. Classes on small colleges are occasionally offered in a variety of graduate programs, and this is also good news. At the end of the day, though, my hope (and that of many other colleagues who work at small colleges) is that the faculty who produce so much of the literature of higher education and student affairs will focus more directly on the work of student affairs practitioners in small college settings. Until then, I hope that readers find this volume to be informative and thought provoking. I especially hope that student affairs colleagues in small colleges see themselves and their experiences reflected realistically.

In addition to my gratitude to Debbie Heida, Douglas Oblander, Janet Heeter Bass, Bruce Colwell, and William Flanagan for their generosity of time and effort, I wish to acknowledge colleagues who have been supportive of this effort. Roberta Larson, Sam Thios, and Carrie Kortegast at Denison University, along with a wonderful group of colleagues from the National Association of Student Personnel Administrators small college and university community, have provided sustained interest in this effort. My thanks go to them as well.

Sarah B. Westfall
Editor

SARAH B. WESTFALL is vice president for student development and dean of students at Kalamazoo College in Michigan.

1

This chapter defines the small college setting and
addresses the historical and current importance of
understanding the work of the small college dean.

Charting the Territory: The Small College Dean

Sarah B. Westfall

Why spend time thinking about the small college dean? Aside from the self-interest of those of us serving as small college deans, there are good reasons to consider this role. If one accepts the premise that student affairs work is interesting and valuable, then small colleges, due to their numbers alone, are a particularly rich vein to mine. This chapter charts the territory of the small college dean by identifying reasons that considering the topic is important, defining small colleges, including their current and historical role in American higher education, and defining the current and historical role of the small college dean.

Why Examine the Small College Dean?

The role of the small college dean is important because the majority of senior student affairs officers (SSAOs) are in small colleges. The 2004 "Digest of Education Statistics" of the National Center for Educational Statistics (NCES) reported that 3,133 of the 4,071 colleges and universities in the United States enroll five thousand or fewer students. This means that 77 percent of American colleges and universities are small colleges. Assuming that nearly all of these institutions have an SSAO, it is safe to assume that approximately three-quarters of all SSAOs are in small college settings.

Small colleges constitute a decidedly diverse group of institutions. Understanding how these differences shape and are manifested in the work of the dean is important for anyone aspiring to serve as dean in a small

NEW DIRECTIONS FOR STUDENT SERVICES, no. 116, Winter 2006 © Wiley Periodicals, Inc.
Published online in Wiley InterScience (www.interscience.wiley.com) • DOI: 10.1002/ss.221

5

college. Focused attention on the work of the small college dean is the single best way to understand how the institutional environment affects this role. It is also essential in understanding how well a particular small college environment matches one's personal and professional values. In many ways, the decision to work at a small college is as much a lifestyle choice as it is a professional commitment.

Within the profession of student affairs itself, the interests of small colleges are coming to the fore in ways they have not previously. The National Association of Student Personnel Administrators (NASPA) has had an active small college group in recent years. Its board and some of its recent presidents have intentionally sought small college representation on the board itself and on various committees. Of NASPA's institutional memberships, 64 percent are from small colleges. NASPA's recognition of this important constituency (and source of income) is timely and reflects the value of a focus on small colleges (National Association of Student Personnel Administrators, n.d.).

Finally, it is important to spend time considering the small college dean because the role is largely absent from the literature. Appleton, Briggs, and Rhatigan's *Pieces of Eight: The Rites, Roles, and Styles of the Dean by Eight Who Have Been There* (1978) includes perspectives from two small college deans. In 1986, Young's "The Small College Point of View: An Ideology of Student Affairs" was published, as was *Private Dreams, Shared Visions: Student Affairs Work in Small Colleges,* edited by Kuh and McAleenan. Young's article suggests that student affairs work in small colleges could be described as an ideology based on sociological models of community. In *Private Dreams,* focused on communicating the value of student affairs work in small colleges, Dodson, Volp, and McAleenan (1986) provide their personal perspectives on work as senior student affairs officers in small colleges. Palm (1985) provides a similar perspective.

More recently, Sandeen's *Making a Difference: Profiles of Successful Student Affairs Leaders* (2001) includes interviews with a small number of small college deans. The publication most directly focused on the work of the small college dean is Tederman's *Advice from the Dean* (1997). He writes from an intentionally nonscholarly perspective as a veteran dean in private liberal arts colleges. Other occasional articles and chapters address student affairs work in small colleges, but a sustained focus on the small college dean is largely absent from the literature.

What Is a Small College? Who Is a Dean?

The technically correct answers to these questions are, of course, "It depends." A campus of twelve thousand students is small compared to Miami Dade College or the University of Minnesota, for example. For our purposes, a small college is one with an enrollment of five thousand or fewer students. There is nothing magical about this size, but it does accord with the new Carnegie classifications and with some other publications on small colleges (Carnegie Foundation, n.d.; Kuh and McAleenan, 1986). In defining small colleges this way, it is important to recognize that many small colleges are very small. Some enroll only a few dozen students. This reminder is helpful in understanding that the range of small colleges is broad.

The dean refers to the senior student affairs officer (SSAO). This position may be titled dean of students, vice president for student affairs, vice president for student affairs and dean of students, dean of campus life, or something similar.

Why Small Colleges Matter

Small colleges play an important role in American higher education. In addition to constituting 77 percent of American colleges and universities, small colleges enrolled 26 percent of all undergraduates in 2002 (National Center for Education Statistics, 2004). Put another way, small colleges constitute a significant majority of institutions of higher education in the United States and educate a quarter of undergraduates.

The history of small colleges is really the history of American higher education prior to the mid-1940s. Before World War II, few institutions in the country had enrollments above five thousand students, and so virtually every college graduate had attended a small college. Most small colleges were founded in the nineteenth century, and many persist today, often in forms that bear notable resemblance to their early days (Rudolph, 1990). Although there is disagreement about the actual number of colleges founded during this time, it is clear that this was a period of growth and expansion, often following rail lines and westward migration. Cheap, plentiful land was available, and the missionary activities of many Christian denominations established numerous small colleges (Brubacher and Rudy, 1976). These church-related institutions have been a mainstay of American higher education since the beginning, with many evolving into nonsectarian, independent institutions. The institutions that have severed their ties with denominational groups over time are examples of the ways in which small colleges have been among the most resilient institutions in the United States. Small colleges have survived by simultaneously adapting to changing societal circumstances and holding on to their traditions.

The essential historical role of small colleges is illustrated by their unique accomplishments: the enduring success of the colonial colleges, the early openness of Oberlin College to coeducation and students of color, the success of graduates of the Seven Sisters and other women's colleges, the unique access afforded by Berea College and other work colleges, the strong traditions established at many historically black colleges and universities, and the commitment to social justice evident at many church-related colleges.

NEW DIRECTIONS FOR STUDENT SERVICES • DOI: 10.1002/ss

A particularly important role that small colleges have played over time is advocacy. The majority of single-sex institutions, historically black institutions, and tribal institutions, as well as many Catholic institutions, are small colleges. These institutions were founded as a way of providing opportunities to students typically excluded from other institutions (many of them also small colleges). The ability of small colleges to respond to societal problems such as discrimination has been a hallmark of American higher education.

Small colleges played key societal roles not only by virtue of their founding, but also by virtue of political movements and significant events that occurred at small colleges. In the early 1990s, for example, Mills College students resisted an initiative to make the women's college coed. Their strong support for maintaining Mills as a women's college was an important affirmation of the value of single-sex institutions to those who have chosen them. The Deaf President Now movement at Gallaudet College in the late 1980s was a significant moment in the history of deaf and hearing-impaired citizens all over the country.

The universe of small colleges is large and highly diverse. Part of this diversity is the distinctiveness that many small colleges have cultivated over time (Shulman, 1974). Many small colleges of a certain type may look similar in terms of enrollment, age, campus location and size, student body characteristics, and faculty characteristics, for example, but it is certain that each institution has characteristics that make it unique. The tradition at Mt. Holyoke College of identifying each class with a color and an animal (Red Pegasus, for example) is an important and distinctive part of the culture for students that is not the same for other women's colleges. The presence of the Greek system at DePauw University is manifested differently than it is at Washington and Lee University, another strongly Greek campus. This diversity has always been present and has increased over time as small colleges adapted to societal pressures (Jonsen, 1978). It is safe to say that institutional distinctiveness, and the diversity resulting from it, is one of the most valuable assets a small college has.

The term *small college* may evoke an archetypal image of a small, private liberal arts college in a bucolic setting. Certainly many small colleges are in such settings, but this image is more romantic than representative. Many institutions, including those represented by some of the authors of subsequent chapters, do fit this image, but it is important to see the diversity of institutions beyond this archetype. Small colleges include elite, well-regarded institutions with tremendous wealth (Grinnell, Pomona, and Wellesley, for example, all have endowments of more than $1 billion). Many other small colleges are what Astin and Lee (1972) term "invisible." These are the places defined as small, private colleges with limited resources. Compared to their elite counterparts, invisible colleges are typically rooted in a strong religious tradition, founded in the mid- to late nineteenth century, are largely tuition driven, and have relatively open admissions policies.

NEW DIRECTIONS FOR STUDENT SERVICES • DOI: 10.1002/ss

Small colleges include public institutions such as the University of Minnesota Morris and Fort Lewis College (Colorado), as well as branch and regional campuses like Penn State Behrend and Arizona State University's Polytechnic campus. These institutions include two-year and four-year institutions, residential and commuter institutions, and colleges that offer graduate degrees. Small colleges, including traditional residential liberal arts colleges, are located in urban and suburban areas as well as rural areas. They offer a variety of curricula, ranging from the traditional liberal arts to fine and performing arts to theology to health professions to trades.

Small colleges include institutions with a wide range of social, political, and religious commitments. Hillsdale College's refusal of federal financial assistance and the concomitant governmental mandates, Gallaudet University's commitment to education for the deaf and hard of hearing, and Principia College's commitment to higher education for Christian Scientists are good examples. There are also many highly specialized institutions, such as law schools, medical schools, schools of chiropractic, seminaries, conservatories, and culinary institutes that are small colleges.

The importance of size has currency beyond the constellation of small colleges. The learning community movement that gained so much momentum in the mid-1990s was in many ways an attempt at creating arguably small college–like characteristics on large college campuses. Some of the principles underlying learning community initiatives include an emphasis on organizing students into small communities where they develop relationships with one another and with faculty members, are supported by collaborative work between academic affairs and student affairs, and become connected to campus resources and innovative teaching in support of their learning (MacGregor and Smith, n.d.).

Another indication that size is an important institutional characteristic is its inclusion, for the first time, in the Carnegie Foundation classifications of higher education institutions. In 1970, the Carnegie Foundation developed the classifications to aid in research on colleges and universities. The past thirty-five years have seen multiple revisions of the classifications, and attention to the setting of colleges and universities is now explicitly part of the classifications. An important component of the setting is, of course, size. "Size matters. It is related to institutional structure, complexity, culture, finances, and other factors. Indeed, it is probably the most influential omitted variable in the 1970 classification framework" (Carnegie Foundation, n.d.). In the new classification system, institutions identified here as small colleges are classified as "very small," "small," or "medium." In the Carnegie classification system, very small institutions, generally, are those with fewer than 1,000 degree seeking students. Small institutions are those with 1,000–2,999 students, and medium institutions are 3,000–9,999 students.

Simply put, small colleges matter because they include a wide range of institutions, have a long history of success and adaptation, and continue to play a central role in American higher education.

NEW DIRECTIONS FOR STUDENT SERVICES • DOI: 10.1002/ss

Historical Role of the Dean

The dean of students in small colleges has played a variety of roles. Originally deans came from the faculty and had primary responsibility for student conduct and discipline. Often they lived on campus or in residence halls, and, along with the rest of the faculty, acted in the place of the students' parents. There is disagreement about when the first true dean of students (usually male students) emerged. Rudolph (1990) suggests that the first deans appeared shortly after the Civil War in response to the dehumanizing effects of university growth and specialization. Brubacher and Rudy (1976) identify the 1890s as the decade that saw the first deans, and Rhatigan's history of the National Association of Student Personnel Administrators (n.d.) pegs 1901 as the year when the first true dean assumed his responsibilities. If colleges and universities truly acted in loco parentis, the person and office of the dean was the entity most directly responsible for parenting students.

Separate roles emerged for deans in coeducational settings sometime later. Deans of women and deans of men often coexisted in the same institution, usually with the dean of men in the superior position. Separate professional organizations grew out of the two roles: deans of women had the National Association of Women Deans and Counselors, and deans of men had the National Association of Deans and Advisors of Men. By 1937 W. H. Crowley, a dean of men, presciently suggested that his position would soon evolve into a broader role titled dean of students (Rhatigan, n.d.).

As small colleges faced competition from large institutions, kept pace with societal changes and expectations, and diversified their student bodies and curricular offerings, administrative roles became more complex. After World War II when campuses had an influx of veterans, deans helped craft programs (like family housing, independent student governance structures, and offices of veterans' affairs) that met the needs of much more worldly and diverse students than had previously been to college. Deans of students in the late 1960s, for example, had to manage student activism related to civil rights, women's rights, student free speech, and the Vietnam War. The federal Family Educational Rights and Privacy Act in 1974 required that universities change their in loco parentis relationship with students. Deans at many single-sex institutions in the 1970s had to navigate the introduction of coeducation when most formerly men's colleges began admitting women. When the population of traditional-aged college students decreased in the 1980s, deans helped colleges develop programs for older and returning students. In recent years, deans have helped institutions respond to government requirements related to drugs and alcohol and crime reporting, for example, as well as strategic decisions shaped by legal findings regarding mental health issues and disabilities. Deans have always been on the front line in helping institutions develop and respond to increasing diversity in the student body.

NEW DIRECTIONS FOR STUDENT SERVICES • DOI: 10.1002/ss

Deans at small colleges have, over time, worn multiple hats and developed numerous areas of competence. Colleagues at large institutions faced many of the same challenges, but have typically had larger staffs to share the burden of increasingly complex work. Deans at institutions with the fewest resources (staff, professional development funds, access to expert assistance) have the same institutional obligations as colleagues at more affluent institutions and face special challenges in meeting these obligations. Tuition-driven institutions are especially sensitive to changes in the very competitive arena of college admissions, for example, and sometimes lose staff positions in student affairs when revenues are down.

One of the significant symbolic changes that has occurred in the past twenty years is the change in the senior student affairs officer title. Dean of students positions have frequently evolved into or added vice president titles. This change is reflective of the increasing complexity of the work and the importance of the role in institutional decision making. Institutional issues that require expertise in student affairs include admissions, retention, compliance with governmental and legal mandates, media relations, crisis preparation and response, and parent relations, to name a few. Especially progressive institutions recognize that student affairs expertise may also have benefits in making curricular decisions (about starting or increasing off-campus-study programs, for example).

The Role of the Small College Dean

The majority of SSAOs in U.S. institutions work in broadly diverse, small college settings. Like most other administrators at small colleges, they serve as generalists with wide-ranging responsibilities and competencies. Depending on the type and financial health of the institution, the dean has varying levels of responsibility for supporting admissions efforts, improving retention (sometimes making sticky ethical decisions along the way regarding if and when to separate students from the institution), and working with parents and families. Many student life policies at small colleges follow from and reflect strong institutional missions and values. In some cases, the values are so influential that only a select group of candidates could effectively serve as dean (Bob Jones University, for example, has a strong fundamentalist Christian identity and retains both a dean of women and a dean of men).

Small college deans typically have small staffs and are relatively accessible to students, families, faculty, and administrative colleagues at their institution. If they are not on the front line in many thorny student life issues, they are often the final arbiter. As an increasingly broad array of students have come to campus, the dean typically takes leadership in responding to changing needs and campus demands. Depending on one's perspective on a given issue, the dean may be viewed as both advocate for and obstacle to change.

NEW DIRECTIONS FOR STUDENT SERVICES • DOI: 10.1002/ss

Small college deans characteristically have comprehensive portfolios, requiring expertise in multiple areas and a willingness to learn about and stay abreast of others. Some of the most dynamic areas for small college deans relate to legal issues (federal, state, and local laws regarding educational records, alcohol, learning disabilities, mental health, and sexual assault, as examples), working with increasingly involved parents, and challenges related to diversity (support services for underrepresented students, accommodations for transgendered students, and the like). Episodic concerns also require the attention of small college deans (food poisoning from the campus dining service, student protests, and campus incivility, for example).

Depending on the setting and location, the dean may play a significant role in fostering town-gown relationships. Colleges with sizable populations of students living in the local community can face special challenges with these relationships, especially if students are not good neighbors. It is almost certain that every small college dean will have central responsibility for managing student crises and emergencies.

The role of a small college dean is significant. Breadth of responsibility and adaptation to change are perhaps the most significant markers of this role.

Conclusion

The small college dean position is one worth understanding because small colleges comprise over 77 percent of all colleges and universities in the United States and have played a central role in American higher education from the beginning. These institutions represent great diversity, both historically and today. The Carnegie Foundation has recently recognized the importance of size in its classification of colleges and universities. Similarly, small college deans comprise the largest number of senior student affairs officers, have broad-reaching responsibilities, and play multiple roles in their daily work. The small college dean is a key student affairs position in many institutions, and time spent understanding the dean's work is important to a fuller understanding of student affairs itself. A helpful result of this consideration of small college deans may be the development of a research agenda for small colleges in general.

References

Appleton, J. R., Briggs, C. M., and Rhatigan, J. J. *Pieces of Eight: The Rites, Roles, and Styles of the Dean by Eight Who Have Been There.* Portland, Ore.: NASPA Institute for Research and Development, 1978.

Astin, A. W., and Lee, C.B.T. *The Invisible Colleges: A Profile of Small, Private Colleges with Limited Resources.* New York: McGraw-Hill, 1972.

Brubacher, J. S., and Rudy, W. *Higher Education in Transition: A History of American Colleges and Universities, 1636–1976.* (3rd ed.) New York: HarperCollins, 1976.

Carnegie Foundation for the Advancement of Teaching. "Size and Setting Description."
     n.d. Retrieved Oct. 2006 from http://www.carnegiefoundation.org/classifications/
     index.asp?key=790.
Dodson, D. P., Volp, P. M., and McAleenan, A. C. "The View from the Top: The Small
     College Student Affairs Officer's Experience." In G. D. Kuh and A. C. McAleenan
     (eds.), Private Dreams, Shared Visions: Student Affairs Work in Small Colleges. Wash-
     ington, D.C.: National Association of Student Personnel Administrators, 1986.
Jonsen, R. W. Small Liberal Arts Colleges: Diversity at the Crossroads? ASHE/ERIC
     Higher Education Research Report, no. 4. Washington, D.C.: American Association
     for Higher Education, 1978.
Kuh, G. D., and McAleenan, A. C. Private Dreams, Shared Visions: Student Affairs Work
     in Small Colleges. Washington, D.C.: National Association of Student Personnel
     Administrators, 1986.
MacGregor, J., and Smith, B. L. "Frequently Cited Goals of Learning Communities." N.d.
     Retrieved May 2006 from http://www.evergreen.edu/washcenter/lcfaq.htm#23.
National Association of Student Personnel Administrators. "Open Letter from Tara
     Knudson Carl." n.d. Retrieved May 2006 from http://www.lclark.edu/org/naspa/flana-
     gan.html.
National Center for Education Statistics, "Digest of Education Statistics, 2004." 2004.
     Retrieved Oct. 14, 2006, from http://nces.ed.gov/programs/digest/d04/tables/dt04_
     169.asp.
Palm, R. P. "Student Personnel Administration at the Small College." NASPA Journal,
     1985, 22(3), 48–54.
Rhatigan, J. J. "NASPA History." n.d. Retrieved May 2006 from http://www.naspa.org/
     about/index.cfm?show=5.
Rudolph, F. The American College and University: A History. Athens, Ga.: University of
     Georgia Press, 1990.
Sandeen, A. Making a Difference: Profiles of Successful Student Affairs Leaders. Washing-
     ton, D.C.: National Association of Student Personnel Administrators, 2001.
Shulman, C. H. Private Colleges: Present Conditions and Future Prospects. ERIC/
     Higher Education Research Report, no. 9. Washington, D.C.: American Association
     of Higher Education, 1974.
Tederman, J. S. Advice from the Dean: A Personal Perspective on the Philosophy, Roles, and
     Approaches of a Dean at a Small, Private, Liberal Arts College. Washington, D.C.:
     National Association of Student Personnel Administrators, 1997.
Young, R. B. "The Small College Point of View: An Ideology of Student Affairs." Journal
     of College Student Development, 1986, 27(1), 4–18.

SARAH B. WESTFALL is vice president for student development and dean of students at Kalamazoo College in Michigan.

2

This chapter provides an overview of functional areas included in the portfolio of the small college dean. Four examples of organizational charts are offered, as well as factors that will influence the small college student affairs portfolio in the future.

The Student Affairs Portfolio in Small Colleges

Debbie E. Heida

> The small college ideology is characterized by synergy, values education, personalized relationships, and organic change.
> R. B. Young (1986, p. 71)

> The diversity of staff and program responsibilities is frequently the most challenging aspect of a dean's work. In addition to the mainstays of student affairs . . . , student affairs work on small college campuses is always carving new directions in response to student interests and needs.
> D. P. Dodson, P. M. Volp, and A. C. McAleenan (1986, pp. 87–88)

The student affairs portfolio for small college deans is influenced by many things: institutional mission, history, resources, strategic plans, and presidential preference, to name a few. This chapter describes some of the factors that influence what is included in the traditional small college portfolio, describes typical portfolios, provides some models of student affairs divisions, and outlines some of the key elements contributing to the evolution of the small college dean's portfolio.

New Directions for Student Services, no. 116, Winter 2006   © Wiley Periodicals, Inc.
Published online in Wiley InterScience (www.interscience.wiley.com) • DOI: 10.1002/ss.222

15

Mission

Small colleges tend to be highly mission driven institutions. This mission adherence is possible because their limited size permits both a clear and compelling mission and an ability to be organized around this mission. On many small college campuses, students, faculty, and staff can talk clearly about their institution's mission and how it contributes to the overall college experience. Campus leaders spend significant time ensuring that the campus creates a unique position in the marketplace, one that is based on historical mission as well as current market realities. This matters because the competition for students is keen. There is little room for error in "making the class" at a campus that depends on tuition revenue for 70 to 80 percent of the campus operating budget. Knowing who you are and what you strive for in clear, certain terms provides clarity to everything from admission decisions to organizational culture and organizing principles for the functions of the college.

Being a senior student affairs officer at a small college requires the ability to serve in many roles at the same time. One serves as advisor, counselor, supervisor, program planner and initiator, crisis manager, strategic thinker, and institutional officer, among other roles. There is frequent interaction with individual students, student organizations, student leaders, students in crisis, or students referred because of conduct issues. Small colleges provide significant opportunity to develop relationships with individual faculty members as well, working together to assist students, serving on committees or task groups, and interacting at campus events and programs. Other constituencies include parents, community leaders, alumni, and board members, in addition to the professional and support staffs who make up the student affairs division and other campus administrative areas.

There is great diversity in the portfolios of senior student affairs officers at small colleges. Functions are often assigned based on the history and mission of the campus. For example, Warren Wilson College, a work college, has a dean of student work. The college's commitment to work as well as the pervasive nature of the program (all students work) gives this position its unique status and a direct report to the president. As another example, the reporting relationship of the campus chaplain or religious life program is sometimes a function of the history of the college and its governing body.

As much as mission shapes organization charts, the personalities and experiences of the members of the senior leadership team also influence portfolios. For example, on a campus where admissions reported to institutional advancement, the vice president for advancement had been the director of admissions, and the college was well served by keeping his talents involved in the enrollment operation.

On small campuses, organization charts tend to be more organic than at larger institutions, making it rare to find organizational charts that remain constant over time. Because the number of units and the staff involved are of a manageable size at small colleges, it is possible to move the reporting relationships around without the disruption found in larger work arenas. Changing strategic initiatives can also have an impact on the organizational structure. New strategic plans may mandate a new way of seeing the college and organizing for the work ahead. New partnerships and alliances can frequently help an initiative make significant progress in a short period of time.

Finally, one of the major influences on portfolios is presidential preferences. With the average tenure of a college president a mere five years (Martin, Samels, and Associates, 2004), it is quite foreseeable that changes in the job descriptions of senior staff would also change frequently. Presidents are the sum of their experiences and will have had the opportunity to work with a variety of organizational structures in their professional lives. They arrive with preferences, and most arrive with a mandate for change in key areas.

Typical Portfolio

Although there is no typical portfolio, several areas traditionally fall within the purview of the senior student affairs offices. I have used a random survey of sixty-five colleges (from *U.S. News and World Report America's Best Colleges* categories: fifteen from the top liberal arts colleges, ten from the third tier, and ten each from the various regional comprehensive institutions) and identified the areas that are most frequently part of student affairs:

• Office of the dean of students. The dean's office may be a separate office from the vice president for student affairs or serve as the office of the senior student affairs officer. The dean is an important part of the student support network, providing counseling and advising support for improving academic performance, addressing behavioral issues, and crisis intervention. The dean serves as a primary referral agent, assisting students in navigating the bureaucracy that exists in even the smallest of schools. The role includes advocacy for individual students and groups of students, education of the campus community about the changing needs of students, and creating partnerships to develop services and programs to meet students' needs. The dean's office may function as an ombudsman in addition to supervising key areas of the student affairs staff.

• Judicial affairs. Responsibility for student conduct was one of the earliest roles for the dean of students. In the early days, the dean handed out consequences for student behavior in a paternalistic way. If there was trouble in town, the dean would be called and would intervene on behalf of the college, the student, and the student's parents. Today's dean's office coordinates a more elaborate conduct process that includes hearing officers, judicial boards, and appeals processes. Honor codes are often under the purview of the dean of students' office in addition to other conduct processes.

• Residential life. If residence halls exist on a campus, responsibility for their management and programs is with student affairs. There is frequently a division in responsibility for staffing, programming, and assignments in one area and the facility management in another. Typically the facility management function falls under physical plant and requires a solid working relationship with the plant staff and the vice president for finance. Setting fees, planning for renovation and new facilities, and day-to-day repair are usually the purview of the plant staff yet require frequent communication and collaboration with student affairs.

The centrality of residence life to the vibrancy of a residential campus frequently results in the use of an associate dean title for this position. One of the most frequent mechanisms that small schools use to stretch their resources is giving collateral assignments to residence hall staffs. Often resident directors have a ten- to fifteen-hour per week assignment in another student affairs area, for example, the residence life central office, student activities, career development, volunteer services, or leadership development.

• Student activities. Student affairs divisions include a unit that focuses on cocurricular programs. There is great variance, however, in the organizational structure of student activities. It is often paired with the student center or student union, Greek life, leadership development, and campus scheduling. Student activities typically coordinates the campus programming board, support for student organizations and their advisors, and the coordination of funding for student activity areas.

• Career services. My own survey of career services indicates that approximately 75 percent of the colleges house career services in student affairs (25 percent are housed in academic affairs). Several of these colleges also include student employment in their career services operations, but the most frequently cited responsibilities are exploration of majors and career interests, externships and internships, job placement activities, and alumni career networks.

• Health services. There is great variety in the types of health services provided by small colleges, with the responsibility for their management assigned to the senior student affairs officer. Some campuses have contractual agreements with local clinics or hospitals, others offer on-campus clinics, and a few still have infirmaries (facilities that are open twenty-four hours a day, seven days a week) on campus. A growing number offer health education programs and a host of services to provide care for students when ill; ongoing treatment for allergies, eating disorders, and sexually transmitted diseases; and other preventive health care needs for students. There is great diversity in the role of physicians with health centers. It is rare to find a full-time physician on a small campus; the percentage of full-time equivalency varies greatly, but most campuses have a physician on campus just a few hours each week. The director of the health center is typically a nurse or nurse practitioner who operates under the direction of the physician for individual health care for students.

• Counseling centers. Counseling centers vary with the size of the campus and the model chosen for providing service. Some campuses provide psychologists, others licensed counselors, and still others a staff member with a master's in social work. Most have some contractual relationships with local psychiatrists or psychologists for supervision of the counseling center when a psychologist is not on staff.

• Greek affairs. On small campuses, oversight for fraternities and sororities is typically not far from the senior student affairs office. The nature of the complex relationship with students, alumni, and national offices in addition to town-gown relationships requires care and attention. On campuses with large Greek systems, the staff member who is directly responsible for fraternities and sororities often carries the title of assistant dean of students. On campuses with smaller populations, the director of Greek affairs often reports to the director of student activities or director of residence life.

• Multicultural student affairs. Support for students of color; diversity education for students, faculty, and staff; and centers that celebrate and educate about the contribution of diverse student populations are essential components of student affairs divisions. On some campuses, this role is housed in the president's office with a dual reporting relationship with student affairs. Larger campuses often have individual staff members who represent the larger populations of minority students (African American students, Hispanic/Latino students, Native Americans, and Pacific Islanders, for example).

• Chaplains and religious life. College chaplains and religious services report to student affairs in nine out of ten campuses when there is a religious or denominational relationship to the college. For campuses without a religious or denominational affiliation, college chaplains reported to student affairs about one-third of the time.

Drawing again from the *U.S. News and World Report* sample of small colleges, the following areas report to student affairs in about half the institutions surveyed:

• Programs for international students. Support for international students who are studying in the United States is typically a student affairs function. If the international programs office is also responsible for study-abroad programs, this office often reports to academic affairs.

• Campus safety and security. Nearly half the time, responsibility for student safety and security falls in student affairs. The other common reporting line is to the vice president for business.

• Women's center. Not all campuses host a women's center. For those that do, about half the reporting relationship are to student affairs and the other half to academic affairs, typically through the women's studies department.

Other areas that frequently (in at least a third of the sample) report to student affairs are:

• Disability services. This area is responsible for college compliance with the Americans with Disabilities Act, as well as academic and other support for students with learning disabilities, physical disabilities, or psychological disabilities.

• Recreation and intramurals. This responsibility is for fitness, recreation, intramurals, and adventure programs.

• Athletics. Intercollegiate athletics frequently encompasses recreation and intramurals.

• Enrollment management. Responsibility for the admission and financial aid functions of the college lies with student affairs in about a third of institutions. The other two most frequently reported reporting lines are to the academic affairs area or as a direct report to the president.

• Academic services. When academic services do not report to academic affairs, the responsibility for tutoring, study skills assistance, and other services that enhance a student's ability to be academically successful resides in student affairs. The registrar's area and first-year programs are frequently part of academic services.

• First-year experience. On nearly a third of the campuses surveyed, first-year-experience offices report to student affairs.

A number of other areas may also report to student affairs:

• Retention. A quarter of the campuses listed retention as part of the responsibility for student affairs. And even when it is not explicitly listed, accountability for retention frequently resides in student affairs. Regardless of its reporting structure, retention is a collaborative effort with academic and student affairs.

• Food services. In 20 percent of the colleges and universities, food services reports to student affairs.

• Summer conferences and events. In about 20 percent of the colleges, responsibility for summer conferences is part of residence life or student activities.

• Parents' programs. One of the responses to "helicopter parents" (the name given to parents whose high level of involvement in their students' lives is characterized by a hovering presence, like a helicopter) and the changing relationships with parents and students is to promote information services and programs that emphasize partnering with student affairs units and faculty to serve students. Often this is an area that is coordinated in conjunction with advancement, particularly the fundraising portion.

• TRIO programs. These federally funded programs designed to motivate and support disadvantaged students (low income, first-generation, and students with disabilities) frequently report to student affairs. Upward Bound is a program helping historically underserved populations (low income and disabled) prepare for college. Other TRIO programs are Talent

Search and TRIO Student Support Services Program (assisting in identifying students and assisting them in applying to college and student support services, providing preparation for college work, tutoring, and support for students who have enrolled).

• Student work. Student work can report to a variety of areas, including financial aid, business services, career development, or serving as its own stand-alone unit. One of the advantages of a linkage to student affairs is an emphasis on the developmental aspects of student work as they relate to major and career planning.

• Gay, lesbian, bisexual, and transgender services. A growing presence on campus is a department or a staff member with responsibility for gay/lesbian/bisexual/transgender programs. These programs and services are often linked to women's centers or diversity services programs.

• Bookstore. On campuses with auxiliaries reporting to student affairs or when the student center or student union management functions report to student affairs, it is not uncommon to find the bookstore as part of the student affairs portfolio.

Student affairs areas that are unique to just one or two institutions included the post office and telecommunications at Agnes Scott College, the Child Development Center at both Hanover College and Evergreen State University, the Theological Exploration of Vocation Center at Davidson College, the Sophomore Year Experience programs at Beloit College and Colgate University, and financial aid (but not admissions) at Franklin and Marshall University.

It is clear that the potential range of areas within the student affairs portfolio at a small college is almost limitless. The distinctive history and needs of each institution, along with institutional resources and the judgment of each dean, will help determine what areas are included in the portfolio in a given institution. These decisions have a significant impact on staffing, a topic addressed in the next chapter.

Titles

The title for the senior student affairs officer varies among small colleges. Regardless of the title of the senior student affairs officer, associate dean of students is the most common title for the subordinate who handles student conduct and residential life or the staff member who acts on behalf of the senior officer when needed and supervises several areas within student affairs. Assistant dean titles are typically used for areas of importance that do not include the supervision of multiple units within the division. If enrollment management is included in student affairs, there is variation with titles, including the use of associate and assistant titles that reward longevity of service as much as job responsibilities.

NEW DIRECTIONS FOR STUDENT SERVICES • DOI: 10.1002/ss

Student affairs divisions in small colleges are typically flat in their organizational structure resulting in the senior student affairs officer having anywhere from five to twelve direct reports. One implication of this structure is the amount of time spent in staff supervision.

Small schools have the benefit of staff members who fall in love with the campus and its mission, enjoy the benefits of the town that is home to the campus, and hence stay for long periods of time. This is particularly true for staff at the associate dean level. With just one or two of these positions and relative stability in the length of time that staff members stay in them, director-level staff members often feel the need to leave an institution in order to move up. One of the benefits of the flexibility in small schools is that senior student affairs officers can often provide a title change and some reorganization to provide more responsibility in order to retain talented staff members.

A unique feature of small schools is the existence of one-person offices. Offices that most frequently have just one professional are student activities, international programs, disability services, multicultural programs, student center, fraternity and sorority advising, and volunteer services. Campuses with a student population that is less than twelve hundred frequently have one-person career centers, counseling centers, and health centers.

Examples of Organization Charts

Figures 2.1 to 2.4 show organization charts representing increasingly complex organizational models. While Figures 2.3 and 2.4 include a larger number of staff and offices than one might find at most small colleges, the nature of the small school student affairs organization is fairly flat. Functionally, even the complex models tend to feel flat in most small college settings.

Funding

Student affairs units are typically funded through tuition and fees. Although several areas fall under the category of auxiliary services, they rarely fully function in this matter. The National Association of College and University Business Officers defines *auxiliary services* in this way: An auxiliary enterprise directly or indirectly provides a service to students, faculty, or staff and charges a fee related to but not necessarily equal to the cost of services. Auxiliary enterprises are generally self-sufficient operations. . . . The distinguishing characteristic of most auxiliary enterprises is that they are managed essentially as self-supporting activities, whose services are provided primarily to individuals in the institutional community rather than to departments of the institution, although a portion of student fees or other support is sometimes allocated to them" (Powell and Associates, 1994, pp. 1193–1194).

On the small college campus, residence halls, food service, and other auxiliaries often provide a significant source of funds for the college's oper-

Figure 2.1. Simple Organizational Model

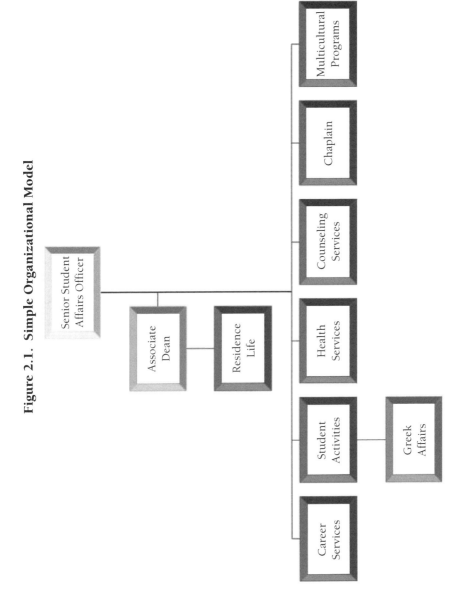

Figure 2.2. Modified Simple Model

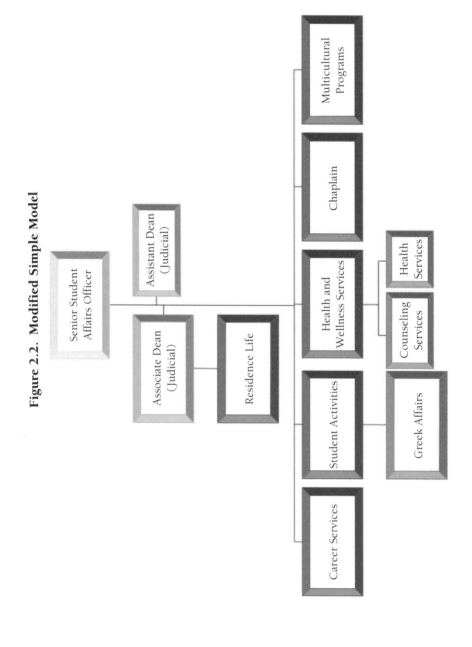

Figure 2.3. Complex Organizational Model

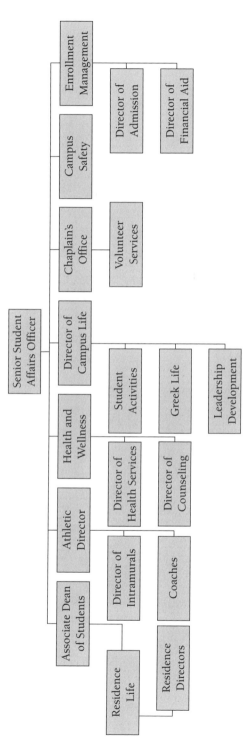

Figure 2.4. Model with Both a Vice President for Student Affairs and a Dean of Students

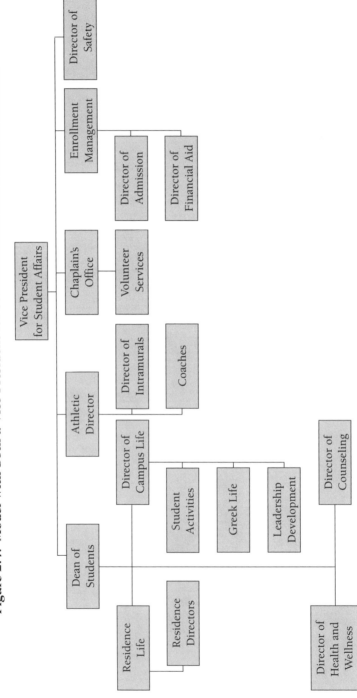

ating budget. It is not unusual for food service to generate $500,000 to $1 million for the college's operating budget. The same is true for residence halls, many of which were built in eras that have long since passed and consequently have been paid off. While this is good news for the college, it does pose limitations on these units. The resources that should be put back into the facilities and the program for future growth are frequently underfunded as the college operating budget needs are more pressing. In addition, the dollars that might be used to fund student affairs positions and programs are typically channeled into the college's general fund.

Evolving Issues in Student Affairs Management

Several trends have changed how student affairs professionals view students, how student affairs functions in small colleges are organized, and how we plan for the future. They include outsourcing some areas within student affairs, the need for services that meet student demands for access twenty-four hours a day and seven days a week, the increasing role of governmental intervention and the need to stay current and prepared to respond to state and federal mandates, and the need to be prepared for campus crises.

In the past ten years, calls for accountability have demanded that campus leaders review the cost-effectiveness of each campus unit and determine its importance to the campus mission. Inherent in this process is asking which services are part of the core mission and which could be provided in a more cost-effective manner by outsourcing the management functions for these areas. Examples of areas that have been outsourced in student affairs are health centers, counseling centers, bookstores, food services, campus safety officers, and housekeeping services in the residence halls. Although outsourcing can sometimes save institutional dollars, the need for managing the quality of the services and students satisfaction with the services remains critical. The major savings to the institution are in the salaries and benefits for the employees within each area. Potential disadvantages of outsourcing include a loss of direct control of the area or service and frequently a change in location for the service itself (for example, counseling services) to an off-campus location, making it less convenient for students to access services. For student affairs divisions, the key is to provide oversight and quality management in ways that meet students needs.

The advent of students' desire for 24/7 access to programs and services has provided the impetus to change many delivery methods for student services. Student affairs divisions are finding what their large school counterparts have known for some time: that a staff member who focuses on technology, database management, and Web development can be helpful in reaching students who would otherwise not be served. These electronic resources also provide services at times that offices are not typically open and staffed. This new technology rarely eliminates the need for personal attention and response on the small campus but serves to supplement what

NEW DIRECTIONS FOR STUDENT SERVICES • DOI: 10.1002/ss

happens in campus offices. The challenge of providing high-tech services along with plenty of personal attention has raised the bar for all those who work in student affairs.

Additional governmental oversight has proven to be positive in providing accountability for students. Students have more open access to information that will assist them in the day-to-day decisions they make about their behavior, safety, and personal information. However, managing everything from the Jeanne Clery Disclosure of Campus Security Policy and Campus Crime Statistics Act to the Patriot Act and responding to the increasingly litigious nature of students and their parents continues to create management challenges for student affairs. Typically many of these areas are handled in the dean's office. The amount of time spent with parents has created stresses in systems that are often staffed with a single staff member who is trying to serve the needs of students.

Finally, the need for campuses to be prepared to respond to a variety of campus crises is providing new leadership opportunities for student affairs. Emergency preparedness has always been an issue, but the need to be ready for everything from terrorist attacks to natural disasters (hurricanes, tornadoes, floods) has prompted special structures on campus. Student affairs plays a critical role in developing protocols to evacuate campus in the event of infectious disease outbreak, responding to regular Student and Exchange Visitor Information System changes for international students, and creating structures that will inform students and their parents of campus services in the event of a crisis.

One other evolving area for student affairs at larger institutions is that of fundraising by student affairs professionals on behalf of the programs and services of their divisions. It is rare to find a small school model that includes someone specifically designated for this function. The creation of strong working relationships with those in institutional advancement has sufficed to date. This will be an area to watch for the future.

Opportunities for Collaboration

Regardless of structure, one thing remains constant: collaboration on campuses. The shifting focus from the campus as a teaching arena to the campus as a learning arena has provided many new opportunities for conversation with those in academic affairs. The assessment movement and the accreditation shift to measuring learning and outcomes rather than inputs have provided impetus for collaboration. First-year-experience programs, sophomore-experience programs, internships, service-learning, parents' programs, retention, student engagement, and academic services all provide unique opportunities to reach out to faculty and involve them in student affairs work. In doing so, the integrated campus environment reaches out to students in ways that ensure that everyone's values and goals are reached by all members of the campus community working together.

NEW DIRECTIONS FOR STUDENT SERVICES • DOI: 10.1002/ss

Conclusion

Student affairs units are some of the most flexible on campus, changing with student and campus needs. The dean's portfolio at small colleges includes a wide variety of departments and services, reflective of individual campuses at particular points in time. As students and external demands change, so do organizational structures. From simple to complex, the organizational chart is ideally a reflection of our commitment to students and their learning. The structure that works today may not work five years from now, and small college deans must be prepared to shift the way they work. Functionally and organizationally, the small college portfolio is filled with opportunities for ever more important cross-campus collaboration.

References

"America's Best Colleges, 2005." *U.S. News and World Report*, 2005.

Dodson, D. P., Volp, P. M., and McAleenan, A. C. "The View from the Top: The Small College Student Affairs Officer's Experience." In G. D. Kuh and A. C. McAleenan (eds.), *Private Dreams, Shared Visions: Student Affairs Work in Small Colleges.* Washington, D.C.: National Association of Student Personnel Administrators, 1986.

Martin, J., Samels, J. E., and Associates. *Presidential Transition in Higher Education.* Baltimore, Md.: Johns Hopkins University Press, 2004.

Powell, D. B. and Associates. "Auxiliary Enterprises and Other Services," *College and University Business Administration*, 3. National Association of College and University Business Officers, 1994.

Young, R. B. "Notes on Student Affairs Administration in the Small College." In G. D. Kuh and A. C. McAleenan (eds.), *Private Dreams, Shared Visions: Student Affairs Work in Small Colleges.* Washington, D.C.: National Association of Student Personnel Administrators, 1986.

DEBBIE E. HEIDA is vice president for student affairs and dean of students at Berry College in Mount Berry, Georgia.

3

This chapter provides an overview of the challenges to and strategies for successful staffing in a small college student affairs division.

Student Affairs Staffing in the Small College

Douglas A. Oblander

One aspect of the small college that requires a great deal of thought and consideration is the area of staffing. The expectations of various stakeholders in a small college require that student affairs staff be versatile, able to function in a variety of settings, and willing to collaborate and that they can seize opportunities that arise and develop relationships easily with a variety of students, faculty, parents, and other staff colleagues.

The recruitment, selection, orientation, training, development, and retention of staff are constant pressures in the small college environment. Some facets of the small college provide incentives for staff to be a part of that setting. As with all other organizational types, however, there are trade-offs among the characteristics that are common to most small colleges. This chapter sketches out the characteristics of the small college as a work environment for both entry- and midlevel professionals, as well as for the senior student affairs officer in such a setting. Although this discussion is not intended to encompass every aspect of staffing or represent the experience of every person working in a small college, it is intended to outline and provoke consideration of relevant issues.

Staffing and the use of staff resources are key elements in student affairs work in small colleges. All of higher education is highly dependent on personnel. In the small college, where relationships and personal attention to students is often the mantra, staffing is crucial.

In many divisions of student affairs, the salary budget is the largest portion of that institutional allocation. When the dean considers the allocation

NEW DIRECTIONS FOR STUDENT SERVICES, no. 116, Winter 2006 © Wiley Periodicals, Inc.
Published online in Wiley InterScience (www.interscience.wiley.com) • DOI: 10.1002/ss.223

of those resources, the issues of effective deployment, staff longevity and development, and the best use of staff to achieve institutional goals may be the most important task. Frequently there are only one or two professionals devoted to a functional area, complicating the issue of how best to staff a particular unit. In that case, effective staffing can define the success of that area or greatly hamper it if the staff members are not functioning in accord with institutional efforts.

Work in a small college is a distinct experience that has opportunities and challenges for both individual staff members and senior student affairs officers who are attempting to develop a division and work within a small college environment. As with any other specific organizational setting, the characteristics of the small college shape the experiences of individuals within that environment. In many cases, the fit between person and organization is important, and perhaps even more so in the small college environment, where relationships can be intense. The size of the pool of potential colleagues can mean that there is a strong orientation toward collaboration and little opportunity to bypass or work around a difficult colleague, an aspect of small college work identified by Hirt, Amelink, and Schneiter (2004).

The need to work with specific persons can require a well-developed set of skills at building relationships and maintaining them. A staff member who performs below acceptable levels or acts in ways that are in conflict with what the organization intends is, at best, a drain on that organization. Not only must other members of the college respond to additional tasks created by an individual's poor performance, it is likely that supervisors will be involved in efforts to correct, monitor, retrain, or perhaps terminate that person. The issue of learning the culture of an institution and developing relationships may be more difficult in the small college, where the roles and the policies may be less formalized than in larger public institutional settings.

In addition, enrollment concerns can drive the planning of many small institutions. Most small college budgets are significantly tuition driven, and therefore the issue of enrollment and retention of students stays near the front of decision makers' concern. The degree to which a division of student affairs or an individual program can demonstrably have an impact on retention or student satisfaction can become part of a powerful argument for their importance to the college.

Significant Responsibility

A relatively new professional can assume significant responsibility early in his or her career due to the flat organizational structure that frequently exists in the small college environment. For example, a new professional in the area of student activities might find that she or he is responsible for organizing and delivering orientation programs and have significant autonomy and budget responsibility in doing so. One of the challenges for young professionals may be that they are thrust into roles for which they are not well prepared. They may also be the only person in their particular role. The redundancy of positions at a large university provides peers with whom a young professional can consult and share experiences.

This level of responsibility and autonomy may require that the new professional quickly learn about both the formal structures and the unwritten or cultural aspects of their environment. In this case, a good definition of what the new staff member needs to understand includes aspects of the campus culture. Culture, as described by Kuh and Hall (1993), is the "collective, mutually shaping patterns of institutional history, mission, physical settings, norms, traditions, values, practices, beliefs, and assumptions which guide the behavior of individuals and groups . . . and which provide frames of reference for interpreting the meanings of events and actions on and off campus" (p. 2). The ability to perceive these often unwritten, but no less crucial, rules can be very important. In particular for new staff members, orientation that includes helping them to understand the culture and prominent actors within it is key. Because many of the programs for graduate education in student affairs or higher education are located in large universities, some staff may not understand the ethos for a small college. As Young (1986) argues, there is no typical small college, but there are some general characteristics that tend to distinguish it from the large university. He contends that the small college is characterized by synergy, values education, personalized relationships, and organic change. In contrast, the large university usually follows an ideology that is much more specialized in quantification and adaptation to societal needs.

The nature of the small college encourages and frequently requires the development of generalists in the field. A common staffing pattern is the combination of work in more than one functional area. A new professional might find that the position he or she holds is a combination of both residence life and student activities, for example. These combinations can add to the quality of a new professional's experience but must be constructed carefully. The combinations should be designed to even out the staff member's work flow and take full advantage of the strengths that person brings to the position. For example, if residence life is part of the position, the beginning of the year can be very busy, so a simultaneous assignment to an orientation program may make the workload difficult to manage.

The ability to work with students in more than one role can add to the depth of a staff member's relationships with students. This can be very positive for getting to know students well and seeing them function in different settings. It can also lead to a degree of familiarity that is difficult to manage, particularly for younger staff members who may not be significantly older than the students.

As Kuh and McAleenan note in *Private Dreams, Shared Visions* (1986):

> Entry level position descriptions at small colleges suggest that student affairs staff should not expect to sleep very much. Jobs are often designed as a combination of two or more halftime positions, such as housing director and

career counselor. The former might include room assignments, student conduct, training and supervision of residence life staff, dorm councils, student
judicial boards, and the usual assortment of activities which comfortably fall
under the heading of "crisis management"; the latter role may include imple-
menting the college's career development program, often without any budget
to speak of. Over the course of the academic year, additional assignments
might be added (for example, study skills class, counseling for students
admitted on academic probation), and it is not unusual to become involved
in student organizations and clubs as well [p. 97].

A generalist must wear many hats; the hats change about every hour,
which can lead to frustration and more than a little pressure. Quick adjust-
ments and unexpected transitions are common; no two days are exactly alike.
This is probably true at large institutions as well, but there is much less specialization in a small college setting that this issue is built into the numerous
roles required of staff. Frustrations aside, playing multiple roles has advantages
because it provides a good sense of the broader student development mission;
permits staff to interact with different types of students and colleagues; and
encourages autonomy, which permits staff to select interesting work to do.

For the young professional who is seeking to collaborate with staff in
other areas and move outside current assignments, the small college provides a wealth of opportunities. Not only is significant responsibility available early in one's career, but also the chance to function autonomously as,
perhaps, the only professional staff member of a one-person office. It is eas-
ier for the successful efforts of the budding star to be recognized in the small
college. Visibility to senior administration and faculty is common in this setting, as staff members are much more likely to find themselves involved in
committees (such as retention, commencement, and task forces) that
encompass all levels of the campus community.

It is also possible to have an impact quickly through program development and innovation. In one small college, for example, a staff member wrote
a proposal for a first-year-experience program for her institution as part of
graduate work in her master's program. The program was adopted by the college, and she became the cocurricular director of the program. Although this
is not always the case, the possibility of a program innovation that can contribute to enrollment and retention is frequently well received in a small college. The opportunity to interact with different populations of students,
participate in institutional governance, and interact with faculty is more likely
in this setting too. This aspect of the small college was identified by Hirt,
Amelink, and Schneiter (2004), who described it in this fashion: "In general,
student affairs administrators at L[iberal] A[rts] C[olleges]s work in environments that encourages creativity and risk taking and where change can be
adopted quickly because bureaucracy is limited. On the other hand, the environment is also political, and faculty members do not seem to understand or
appreciate the work that student affairs administrators perform" (p. 104).

NEW DIRECTIONS FOR STUDENT SERVICES • DOI: 10.1002/ss

Faculty Versus Student Affairs: A Blurred Distinction

The experience of many small college student affairs professionals is that the chasm between them and the classroom faculty is not as distinct as it is in research-oriented institutions. The focus of small college faculty on teaching and student success tends to heighten the faculty's appreciation of the role student affairs plays in the students' education and success at the college. Tederman (1997) contends that faculty should be involved as part of all significant student life–related policymaking committees. He also argues that it is the role of the senior student affairs officers (SSAOs) and others in the student affairs division to help faculty understand student affairs philosophy and how the work of division staff complements the mission of the college.

Encouraging staff to be involved in faculty governance and attend coffee hours and other informal opportunities for interaction are important to establishing relationships with faculty colleagues. Student affairs staff members who have worked only in large institutions will find a new element in their relationships with faculty. Because of smaller class sizes in many small colleges, faculty know the students they teach. It is not uncommon for faculty to ask student affairs staff about an individual student. The faculty member may have had a conversation that leads him or her to think there is an issue with the student where student affairs can help. It is also likely for faculty to call the student affairs staff and ask if they have any knowledge about why a student has not been attending class. This is a common practice and can be an aid to retention. Following up on these requests from the faculty is a visible way for student affairs staff to demonstrate their value to the community and build relationships with individual faculty.

In many cases, long-time faculty members will be very involved as advisors to student organizations. In that role, they can be both a help and a hindrance. For the new staff member in student activities, seasoned advisors may not be receptive to initiating new polices related to student organizations (like requirements for posting, expectations for attending training for treasurers, or advisor training). Those long-term advisors can be a resource in learning what has happened in the past. Faculty advisors may be receptive to building learning opportunities into the structure of student organizations if they understand how these opportunities foster the living-learning environment of the campus.

Close Contact with Key Decision Makers

Professionals in the small college may find they have access to key decision makers on campus, unlike their colleagues at larger universities. While the president of a large university may not come into interpersonal contact with staff except on rare occasions, the small college encourages and often requests it. If the president or academic dean has lunch in the dining commons, this can be seen as positive in the campus community. Similarly, the presence of senior administrators at student events is much more likely at

NEW DIRECTIONS FOR STUDENT SERVICES • DOI: 10.1002/ss

a small college. The young professional may be advising student groups and is often present at the same events attended by senior-level administrators. Planning for homecoming, parents' day, alumni weekend, and a myriad other events may thrust the student affairs professional (student activities, housing, and scheduling, for example) directly into contact with senior administrators and staff.

Relationships with Students

Staff relationships with students in the small college setting often entail knowledge of multiple facets of a student's life. The same student on a small college campus may be a resident assistant, chair of the student activities council, and a member of an academic honor society. The Greek advisor who works with fraternity and sorority presidents has a significantly different interaction with ten chapters than if she or he were working with thirty.

Many small colleges tend to be residential in nature, adding to the opportunities to interact with students. Indeed, the requirement for students to live on campus for a number of years (even four years) is common. The growth in apartment and independent-style housing operated by small colleges is an example of how they are attempting to maintain the positive aspects of their residential nature while responding to the needs of students. In short, staff contacts with students in a variety of capacities, including an extensive residential experience, can create an environment for especially substantive relationships with students.

Relationships with Faculty

The opportunity to work with faculty as colleagues in the campus community is enhanced in the small college. Many small institutions are located in rural or suburban settings that encourage interaction both on and off campus. In addition, the faculty at small colleges tend to place a higher value on campus community than do those at large universities. This is facilitated by the fact that the size is manageable for communitywide events. As opposed to a faculty senate, for example, perhaps the whole faculty meets regularly. Participation in these events can add to the visibility of student affairs staff and increase the number of faculty with whom they become acquainted. The opportunity to collaborate with faculty is often very much a function of relationships that are built in a variety of settings. In some cases, the involvement of faculty is crucial to developing new initiatives. In the case of the first-year-experience program I have already noted, a committee was developed with a faculty chair who was supportive of the idea. Absent his involvement and that of other faculty on the committee, the academic component of that experience would not have been well supported by the faculty and would have been largely unsuccessful.

NEW DIRECTIONS FOR STUDENT SERVICES • DOI: 10.1002/ss

Challenges

The nature of small college work also includes challenges and limitations for staff. In many cases, the salary and benefits may not have kept pace with those in large universities. Successful small colleges may have more opportunity to recognize and reward the contributions of an individual staff member. While the large public institution receives a significant portion of its resources from the state (in a political arena where higher education must compete with many other funding needs), the small college that is successful in enrollment management and fundraising can be more in control of its own fate. When a small college becomes more successful in its enrollment and retention goals, resources become available for program enhancements. It is also likely to result in funding for additional faculty and staff, as well as, in some cases, added compensation for current personnel. The degree to which student affairs staff can add to the success of the institution in these areas may increase the resources available to them.

A good example of an effort that would be well received is one of the recommendations made by Kuh and Associates (1991): that colleges establish early warning systems for identifying students in difficulty. These systems, which identify students with problems and, in collaboration with faculty members and students, form safety nets for them, allow student affairs staff to be centrally involved in an initiative that is important to the college and to develop relationships with faculty.

Building on this idea of collaboration, new faculty members could be contacted by the senior student affairs officer by letter prior to their arrival and in person by a senior member of the student affairs staff soon after they come to campus. During these contacts, held when new faculty are looking for behavioral cues in their environment about what is important, programs and services available on the campus to help students—and to help faculty help students—can be described. At the same time, student affairs staff members establish relationships with new faculty members, who now have a contact in student affairs to whom questions can be addressed and students referred.

Small colleges that are located in rural or suburban settings may have fewer career opportunities for a professional who has a partner or spouse whose work is also in higher education. Such a location can also add to the fishbowl nature of the work. In my experience, in a city of fewer than fifty thousand people, the visibility of college staff can be high. To hear one's neighbors walk by your house and say, "He works for the college," adds a level of pressure even at home. The pressure comes from a high level of visibility and an accompanying loss of privacy and anonymity.

The isolation of these locations may also limit traditional professional development opportunities. Access to airports as well as long distances to state and regional meetings can be a challenge. In addition, the amount of resources allocated for professional travel may be less for small colleges, particularly for younger staff. However, what resources are available may be

NEW DIRECTIONS FOR STUDENT SERVICES • DOI: 10.1002/ss

more flexibly spent. The absence of state rules for travel and reimbursement may allow money to be more effectively used. In many independent institutions, budget management has fewer restrictions, with the budget manager needing only to complete the year with a positive balance. The way in which resources are allocated within that budget may be much more at the discretion of the budget manager.

Within the division of student affairs at a small college, there may be limited mobility. The organization will likely be flat, with few opportunities to stay within the college while advancing in position. A common organizational structure has a new professional reporting to a director or assistant or associate dean who in turn reports to the SSAO. In effect, if a new professional wants to make a significant move upward in responsibility, a director must move on from his or her current position. If a director or associate or assistant dean wants to move, the only chance may be when the SSAO moves or retires. While some staff members are able to accomplish these moves internally, the opportunities more frequently occur as a result of serendipity than planning. The way in which a staff member can prepare is to avoid leaving opportunity to chance. The staff member who seizes the availability to cross-train in other functional areas and is visible to the campus community may be well positioned to be a good candidate for positions that become available.

In many small colleges, there is a belief, particularly among long-time faculty and staff, in the uniqueness and distinctiveness of their college. It is common to hear the phrase, "We are the best-kept secret in the [South, Midwest, or West, for example], or the phrase, "There is a special feel to this place that is hard to quantify." This feeling among people who are in a position to influence hiring decisions can be an advantage to an internal candidate. The organizational culture of a small college will be more easily negotiated by the person who already has some understanding of both place and people.

The lack of opportunities to advance professionally leads to significant turnover, particularly among entry-level staff. For midlevel staff (directors, assistant or associate deans), this means that training and acculturation of new staff are very important. In a study of the socialization of new professionals in student affairs, Oblander (1990) identified several important issues to consider. New professionals found out about the organizations they had entered through interaction with current staff, not always their direct supervisors or others responsible for formally training them. In fact, they often found peer mentors who assisted them in making sense of the organization and its practices. The use of an "insider coach" who is not the supervisor was very helpful. Learning about the organization begins as early as the recruitment process but is rarely addressed intentionally.

Preparation for this likely phenomenon is important in the planning and allocation of resources. Some of the following recommendations may be useful to consider:

- Consider the socialization experiences that newcomers encounter.
- Examine the recruitment process used and the messages that are given to newcomers.
- Ask about and understand newcomers' previous experiences and education.
- Analyze the organization's culture, and determine the major components to be communicated.
- Create nonjudgmental opportunities for newcomers to seek clarification.
- Caution insiders about communicating aspects of the culture that are self-limiting for the organization.

Carefully considering how new staff learn about the organization and how to assist that process are important not only for entry-level staff but also for new midlevel staff.

Visibility

The visibility of staff on a small campus can provide an opportunity to display their talents and willingness to be part of the college. In this way, they may be more readily recognized for the contributions they make. The small college is an organizational setting where staff members' decisions and actions are often plainly on display. The less attractive side of this aspect of the small college is that failures and embarrassing moments are more visible to the entire campus. The failure of a program or a student crisis will be much more visible to the entire campus community in a small college setting. Faculty who are concerned about teaching and student success will have higher expectations that student affairs professionals will be able to address student issues. The issues that occur are more likely to attract the attention of senior college officers who often know the individual students involved. Student government and other student leaders will have significantly more access to presidents and vice presidents than at large universities.

The singular nature of a staff member's responsibilities within the college can create a sense of isolation. A young professional may be the only person with her or his responsibilities within the college. If she or he were in a large institution, there might well be several people with similar responsibilities in the areas of student activities or housing, for example. This creates a convenient, natural support group of colleagues who face similar challenges and can discuss them without the repercussions of showing frustration with supervisors. The need to have peers, or at least nonsupervisory personnel, with whom to process the issues they face can be very important to new professionals in their entry to and understanding of a new organizational culture (Oblander, 1990).

Professional Development

Two other areas are challenging in the small college. The budget and the plan for formal staff development are frequently not as well developed as at large universities. The responsibility for staff development may be part of the portfolio of several staff members or a committee, and will compete for staff time with the rest of those professionals' tasks. The individualized nature of each person's job description may make it more difficult to develop programs that are beneficial to a large portion of the staff.

Access to academic programs to pursue terminal or advanced degrees may be limited for staff members working in small colleges. The highest degree offered at many small colleges is the master's degree. The opportunity available to staff at a large university to work and pursue a terminal degree simultaneously is seldom available to small college staff members without leaving their employing institution and commuting to a larger university.

One of the ways in which some small colleges have addressed several of the issues that are part of small college work is to extend the networking of staff beyond the confines of their own college. Encouragement and support of staff involvement in state and regional professional organizations can provide networking and professional development opportunities at minimal cost in terms of both travel money and staff time.

Some deans have found it very effective to develop one-day exchanges with similar institutions. In this model, a dean and a number of staff members travel to a similar campus for a one-day schedule that might include a joint staff development session (a common reading on a topic in the field with a presentation or discussion), the opportunity to tour facilities on the host campus, and time for staff with similar functional responsibilities to meet together and share ideas. This can be effective for individuals within the staff and has the potential to spur division-wide efforts or discussion of change.

Strategies for Recruitment

The crucial nature of staff in the small college division of student affairs makes the recruitment of quality staff imperative. Staff who not only are professionally competent but understand or can come to understand the issues and challenges they will face at a small college are essential. Many of the larger, well-known graduate preparation programs are located in large, public universities. How does the senior student affairs officer of a small college find the staff she or he needs?

When the opportunity exists, a small college can establish a relationship with a graduate program whereby graduate students are employed part time at a small college within driving distance of the university where they are seeking a degree. This can be beneficial for both institutions. The graduate institution gains financial support for its students, as well as additional sites where students can gain practical experience. The opportunity for students to compare and contrast two different types of institutions can enrich their graduate education. The nature of the small college means that graduate students employed there are able to have significant professional experience in their assistantships. One of the best-developed arrangements of this type is at Bowling Green State University in Ohio. The university has a history of placing its graduate students (particularly at the master's level) in a variety of institutions within about a two-hour radius of campus.

Even if the relationship cannot be as well developed as this example, there are options. The dean might occasionally teach a class at a nearby program or guest-lecture on a specific topic in graduate courses. One of the opportunities might be to share with graduate students what the small college student affairs experience is for new professionals. If location makes it possible, being open to graduate student involvement in the campus through internships and practica can be a chance to get to know prospective staff and see how they work. It can also be an opportunity for graduate students to learn about small colleges and, in particular, the college and people where they intern. This experience may yield a far more knowledgeable new staff member than the traditional interview process.

Another recruitment strategy plays directly to a strength of the small college. The recruitment of staff at the bachelor's degree level of preparation can be an effective way to find young staff. Job descriptions and organizational charts need to reflect the lack of professional preparation that young staff members bring to the table, but the institution also needs to recognize the tremendous energy and enthusiasm these colleagues can bring to the position and the college. The strong, multifaceted relationships that student affairs staff have with students is a way in which potential bachelor's-level staff members can be identified.

It has long been a practice of admissions offices to use recent graduates, and even in the literature on community service and service-learning there is a thread of discussion about the use of "green deans." These recent graduates are usually hired on completion of a bachelor's degree to work with a particular program like community service. Candidates have been strong student leaders and highly involved in the programs they are working with as new professionals. Their knowledge of the college as well as their enthusiasm allows them to contribute immediately. Their tenure may be for only a year or two and is not necessarily in an area where they see themselves working professionally for an extended period of time.

This kind of "grow your own" model for staffing can be very helpful, especially in areas like residence life and student activities. The need for preservice training and orientation becomes paramount in helping these recent graduates make the transition from student to professional staff. Typically they also need significant supervisory assistance and in-service preparation.

NEW DIRECTIONS FOR STUDENT SERVICES • DOI: 10.1002/ss

The more traditional recruitment of staff through conferences, Web sites, and placement exchanges can also be a resource in recruiting talented staff members. Highlighting the strengths of the small college experience, collateral job responsibilities, flexibility and collaboration, and the promise of broad experience early in the person's career at the institution can work to ensure applicants who will be a good fit for the college.

Strategies for Retention

One of the opportunities to aid in retention of staff is the high degree of involvement that they may have in campuswide efforts. For the staff member who is asked to represent the student affairs division on the assessment committee or the retention task force, for example, this can be an enriching experience. Similarly, the opportunity to initiate programs and projects is more available to staff at a small college if funding is available. However, a pilot project that has an impact on as few as a hundred students may be initiated with little cost. Such a pilot program might represent 3 to 5 percent of the total student population or more.

The chance to work in a variety of areas can be a strong incentive for a staff member to continue at a small college. Those who aspire to the role of senior student affairs officer may see this as an opportunity to gain experience in a variety of functional areas early in their career. In addition, the enterprising staff member who seeks and takes advantage of these opportunities will be better positioned for whatever internal promotions develop within the college.

In addition to serving on committees within the college, the enterprising dean may look for ways to adjust staff members' job responsibilities. Lateral moves within the organization or enabling staff to pursue interests within the college are options that can be stimulating for staff. The advantage of the small college is that there are seldom offices that are not in need of additional assistance, and the flexibility to allow this to happen usually exists. In the small college there are generally less well-defined categories of employee classification, and staff members are less likely to be unionized. This fact provides many opportunities for creativity in helping staff develop new skills and competencies.

The characteristics of small college staffing can affect the roles and the position of the dean. She or he will find that the staff is often composed of a much larger percentage of younger staff. This may entail a more significant amount of time spent on supervision and training issues. The increased turnover in the small college can also add to time that needs to be spent on tasks related to training and supervision. There will be few seasoned professionals in student affairs with whom she or he can relate. The opportunity to share experiences and process issues with colleagues may be limited due to the youth or inexperience of the staff. There is an expectation that

SSAOs will have knowledge and expertise in a variety of areas related to students, but this expectation can be difficult to meet.

The other issue in this role is the conflicting pressures for the SSAO between the demands of institution-wide responsibilities and those that are focused on individual student needs. It is not uncommon for the SSAO to be titled as both the vice president for student affairs and dean of students. At different times of the year, the demands of one role or the other can become more pressing. This topic is addressed in Chapter Four, but bears mentioning as a dimension of the staffing that is common to the small college.

Conclusion

The effective use of human resources in student affairs is a crucial issue. This concept is not new to anyone. In one of the most widely read books on organizations in recent history, *In Search of Excellence: Lessons from America's Best Run Companies,* Peters and Waterman (1982) argued for the importance of being "brilliant at the basics" (p. xiii). The people who staff divisions of student affairs make a difference in the quality of our work and our students' experience.

In *Improving Staffing Practices in Student Affairs* (1997), Winston and Creamer contend that the essential values of student affairs—commitment to human dignity, equality, and community—should guide our daily interactions with staff and should guide our actions as we make staffing decisions. They argue that those values should be engaged as we work through what they identify as the five key components of staffing practice: recruitment and selection, orientation to new positions, supervision, staff development, and performance appraisal. The lesson to be taken from these and other authors is that there are few, if any, decisions that are made that do not have staffing implications. As a resource that may be increasingly limited, the decision about how and where to deploy staff is crucial to the planning and success of small colleges in the advancement of learning through their divisions of student affairs.

References

Hirt, J. B., Amelink, C. J., and Schneiter, S. "The Nature of Student Affairs Work in the Liberal Arts College." *NASPA Journal,* 2004, 42(1), 94–110.

Kuh, G. D., and Associates. *Involving Colleges: Successful Approaches to Fostering Student Learning and Development Outside the Classroom.* San Francisco: Jossey-Bass, 1991.

Kuh, G. D., and Hall, J. E. *Cultural Perspectives in Student Affairs Work.* Lanham, Md.: American College Personnel Association/University Press of America, 1993.

Kuh, G. D., and McAleenan, A. C. (eds.). *Private Dreams, Shared Visions: Student Affairs Work in Small Colleges.* Washington, D.C.: National Association of Student Personnel Administrators, 1986.

Oblander, D. A. "Socialization of New Student Affairs Professionals." Unpublished doctoral dissertation, Indiana University, 1990.

Peters, T. J., and Waterman, R. H. *In Search of Excellence: Lessons from America's Best-Run Companies.* New York: Warner Books, 1982.

Tederman, J. S. *Advice from the Dean: A Personal Perspective on the Philosophy, Roles, and Approaches of a Dean at a Small, Private, Liberal Arts College.* Washington, D.C.: National Association of Student Personnel Administrators, 1997.

Winston, R. B., and Creamer, D. G. *Improving Staffing Practices in Student Affairs.* San Francisco: Jossey-Bass, 1997.

Young, R. "The Small College Point of View: An Ideology of Student Affairs." *Journal of College Student Personnel,* 1986, 27, 4–18.

DOUGLAS A. OBLANDER is vice president for student affairs and dean of students at Mount Union College in Alliance, Ohio.

NEW DIRECTIONS FOR STUDENT SERVICES • DOI: 10.1002/ss

4

This chapter examines the role of vice president for student affairs and dean of students, the similarities and differences between the two roles, and the realities of holding both titles at a small college.

Vice President for Student Affairs and Dean of Students: Is It Possible to Do It All?

Janet Heeter Bass

Senior student affairs officers (SSAOs) at colleges and universities carry titles as diverse as the many institutions they represent. Although the literature about the senior role, especially at small colleges, is limited, some research suggests that the role and scope of the SSAO position at small colleges can be affected by such factors as the personality of the president, religious affiliation, location of the campus, and size of the endowment (Palm, 1985; Tederman, 1997). SSAOs are called vice president for student affairs, vice president for student development, or vice president for student services. These officers are also titled dean of students, dean of student development, or dean of student life. At some colleges, one person carries both titles. This chapter focuses on the difference between these two roles and the ways in which SSAOs carrying both titles manage their roles.

At a recent gathering of small college deans, I asked some of my colleagues there what they perceived the difference was between the roles of dean of students and vice president of student affairs. Regardless of the title of the professional responding to this question, there were clear and distinct differences in what assumptions were made about each role. When responding about the responsibilities of the vice president, colleagues mentioned a global perspective, long-range planning, institutional perspective versus division perspective, and fiscal management. A number of colleagues felt that they were granted a greater level of respect by the faculty and other

NEW DIRECTIONS FOR STUDENT SERVICES, no. 116, Winter 2006 © Wiley Periodicals, Inc.
Published online in Wiley InterScience (www.interscience.wiley.com) • DOI: 10.1002/ss.224

community members because they carried the title of vice president. The dean of students title was characterized by terms like *student advocate, day-to-day operations, student governance,* and *staff supervision.* This title was perceived as positive to use with parents and students, because the title of dean was clearer to them than a vice president title.

A number of colleagues who serve as the SSAO believe that their presidents either added vice president to their title or did not have a person titled vice president for political or economic reasons (Council of Independent Colleges listserv, fall 2005). Walker, Reason, and Robinson (2003) found that the mean salary of the professional who carried the title of SSAO was $104,302, while the mean salary of the professional entitled dean was $70,621. This research suggests that the difference in title carries with it an increase in salary opportunities.

Differences in the Two Roles

In exploring the functional differences between the role of dean and of vice president, it is helpful to remember the comments of Bruce Johnston, a colleague at Lyon College. He said, "The person in either position should assume the mind-set of an educator. In the dean's role, that means educating students, faculty, parents, other campus colleagues, trustees, alumni, and community members to the value of cocurricular learning and growth as significant dimensions of the educational experience within the way of collegiate living" (Johnston, personal communication with the author, October 2005). No matter what hat we are wearing or what titles we carry, we should always remember our role in educating others about what we do with and for students.

So what is the difference, if any, in the focus of an SSAO's job as reflected by the title of vice president or dean of students?

For the past ten years, I have served in the role of SSAO at my small college. I started as a dean of students and, resulting from a change in presidential leadership, was also appointed as vice president for student affairs. As I look back, my job did not change significantly due to my title change, but it did change due to the direction and focus of the president. As numerous colleagues noted, the perceptions of my level of authority changed both internally and externally on using the vice president title. I do use both titles but often choose one or the other depending on the situation. At my institution, students are more responsive when they are talking to the dean of students, yet for external issues I usually identify myself as the vice president. The reality is that SSAOs who carry both titles may find juggling the different roles to be difficult.

A vice president must function within the collegial environment in a manner that is different from that of a dean. Individual and group meetings become the norm, and interactions with students are less and less likely to occur. Several years ago, my son was working in our central student life office in August, and one day my husband asked him what he thought about working there. Granted this was August, when the rest of my staff was busy (and, literally, running around) getting residence halls ready, preparing manuals, welcoming early arrivals, and so on. His response to my husband was, "Well, Mom's staff works really hard. All she does is walk in and out and go to meetings." At first I was offended. After all, August is not a bowl of cherries for me either. But then I realized that he never saw me doing what he perceived as "work." While my staff members were dealing with the day-to-day operations of getting ready for another academic year, I was in senior staff meetings working on campuswide issues and presidential directives.

To examine the difference between the vice president role and the dean role, I found myself looking to my own position and what happens on a daily basis. The week prior to the beginning of school and the first week of school provide an excellent opportunity to examine what a SSAO spends time doing and how it relates to the different roles as the vice president and as the dean of students.

Earlier in this chapter, small college SSAO colleagues characterized the differences between the vice president and dean roles by associating specific terms with each role. Those characterizations organize the following practical examples of differences in the two roles over a couple of weeks in the life of an SSAO.

For a vice president, the following might be observed the week before school starts and the first week of classes:

• Global perspective. Participation in meetings regarding the rise in natural gas prices, health insurance, and, as the vice president charged with special events, the coordination of a thirteen-state governors' conference cosponsored by the college. Many hours are spent on the economy, market realities of coming change demographics in the student population between ages eighteen and twenty-two, and government support, or lack of support, for students attending college.

• Long-range planning. Significant time is spent with other vice presidents on such issues as developing student housing options that fit into the college's long-range plan, academic program development at the graduate and undergraduate levels, and reviewing the strategic initiatives developed by the president and senior leadership team.

• Institutional perspective versus divisional perspective. As the SSAO, one's presence is expected at numerous state-of-the-college addresses presented by the president, meetings with new faculty on campus, and spending time with architects who are designing the next building (which, as a dean, I would like to make much bigger but as a vice president, I recognize we cannot afford).

• Fiscal management. Hours are spent on the college's fiscal plan and, in recent years, managing the endowment draw, working on fundraising, and writing grants for major foundations. One of our key interests as a college is diversification of the revenue stream. Many hours are spent discussing how to protect the quality of our undergraduate program and experience while examining other ways in which to enhance revenue.

These issues are all important and critical to the success of the college, but they are not activities that provide many SSAOs with a sense of accomplishment and engagement with students.

The dean of students deals with other issues during this same time of the academic year. Again, I reflect back on the words my colleagues used to describe the position of dean:

- Student advocate. SSAOs often find venues in which they may meet with students to talk about upcoming issues and concerns. For example, I meet with our football team to talk about campus expectations, with our student programming chair and the resident assistants to talk about their focus for the year, and with a fraternity about creating a plan for success. Many SSAOs address the first-year class during orientation to let them know that we are here to help them succeed. As at many other colleges, my division hosts numerous dinners and socials that I attend to try and get to know as many students as possible.

- Day-to-day operations. This involves significant interactions with our physical plant to make sure residence halls are ready for opening, coordination of first-year orientation programs with academic affairs, and meeting with staff about their concerns, ranging from lack of office space to budgets. SSAOs often meet with parents and students who appeal everything from their meal plan to pending judicial sanctions and who insist on "meeting with the dean."

- Student governance. Although most SSAOs have a staff member who advises student government, it is important to meet with the student government president to discuss his or her issues and goals for the year. This may be especially important in institutions where students serve on the board of trustees. Meeting with fraternity and sorority presidents and members of other organizations on campus about their views on current climate and culture helps establish the tone for the year, and I have found it helpful to have a student affairs advisory council that meets with me on a biannual basis to provide feedback about the campus community.

- Staff supervision. This is one of the most critical areas for a dean. Many of us at small colleges experience significant staff turnover. We may often have additions to our staff from other areas of campus. This requires a lot of time educating staff and reinforcing the basic premise of our field: we are here to support and enhance the academic experience and create an environment where students can succeed. Young staff members have developmental needs and often want (or need) ongoing interaction and support as they manage their areas. It is important to establish ways in which staff can meet with the SSAO in one-on-one sessions, small team meetings, and as an entire division.

NEW DIRECTIONS FOR STUDENT SERVICES • DOI: 10.1002/ss

These lists, which are not exhaustive, provide a glance at some of the differences one might experience in reflecting on life as a vice president and as a dean. On a small campus, it becomes an even greater challenge as many of these events and meetings are happening within the same day or even within minutes of each other. One might walk out of a three-hour meeting on writing a grant to fund a major building and into a meeting with frustrated students who feel that campus police are overly zealous.

A personal example of this happened one fall. I was sitting with our president and members of our board of trustees at a football game when I heard a young man behind me bemoaning to his buddy that he was passing the classes he could afford to buy the books for, but was struggling in two other classes for which he could not afford the books. Our staff happens to have a loaner library, so I moved away from the president and our guests and went up to speak with the young man about some options he might not have been aware of that were available to him. When he came to our office the next Monday, I assigned a staff member to work with him, and his academic work subsequently improved. My role at the game was that of a vice president hosting our board members, but I never take off my dean of students hat or opt not to respond to students when appropriate. The concept of multitasking takes on new meaning when two arguably different roles are being played.

Balancing the Roles of Vice President for Student Affairs and Dean of Students

So what does one gain or lose by holding the titles of both vice president and dean of students? One benefit is that one gains a unique perspective about the campus community and one's role in shaping not only the student affairs division but also the entire college. For example, a vice president sits in meetings and talks about program development focused on the incoming class for the coming year. Our campus is currently engaged in a comprehensive campaign, as are many other colleges. As a result, a significant amount of time is spent educating faculty, students, and staff about the concept of intergenerational equity as it relates to fundraising, the travel schedule of the president, and changing the culture of our campus concerning the area of fundraising.

As the vice president, one quickly learns that the college is a complex organization that is a business as well as an educational institution. This is a difficult shift for some people to make as they are looking at resources for their division on campus. The dean of students might want to renovate the residence halls, but the vice president understands the fiscal reality of increasing costs of health insurance, natural gas, and other factors beyond our control. These issues can change the focus of the institutional budget, and one quickly recognizes the business aspects of the college sometimes become paramount.

One of the challenges in carrying the titles of both vice president and dean of students lies in the time it takes to do it all. If the vice president is

NEW DIRECTIONS FOR STUDENT SERVICES • DOI: 10.1002/ss

in meetings the majority of the day, then what clearly is lost is the interaction, both active and passive, in the lives of the students and, sometimes, staff members. It is imperative to intentionally think of ways to be with students that do not always have to be structured. SSAOs have to work to attend at least one sporting event for each varsity sports team, plays, and musical productions and go to dinners or socials at student programs or Greek houses when invited. Some campuses are designed with a commons area, where students gather between classes. I intentionally take my breaks during the class break periods and walk through this crowd of students on campus. One reason is to let students see me and give me a chance to talk to different students. It also makes me happy. I like our students, and their energy and enthusiasm is what makes me love my job.

Connections with students (and their energy and enthusiasm) can be a casualty of work as a vice president, and good SSAOs take time to cultivate contact with students. This is a special challenge for SSAOs who are carrying both titles where close student relationships are an expectation of the position.

Getting It Done

So what is the reality of having these titles on a small campus? Can you do it all? Probably not. A friend once said, "Perfection is the enemy of the good." I am not perfect, and I do not expect my staff, my students, or even the president to be perfect either. Fortunately I work for a president who does not expect perfection; she does expect a bias for action. As a result, I strive to surround myself with good staff members who are engaged and excited about what they do and enjoy working in the environment we have on campus. I am able to accomplish what I do because of them, and I recognize them as part of the team that helps me succeed as the vice president and dean of students.

The relationship with the president is one of utmost importance to the SSAO, regardless of title, and that should be communicated throughout the division. It is important in the development of the day-to-day life of the campus that the student affairs staff knows what the mission of the college is and where it is going. Just as important, the staff needs to understand the current focus of the college as an institution. At some colleges, this means retention, and at others it is assessment. Some colleges are happy with their current number of students; others want to grow. Whatever the case may be, it is the SSAO's responsibility to make sure the focus of the division is in line with the vision of the president and the board of trustees. This is not to say, however, that staff time and effort should not continue to go toward the traditional efforts of our field. It means that, for some, the work of the division will shift as institutional priorities change.

Whether the senior student affairs officer is called dean or vice president, one thing is clear: if the position reports to the president, it often comes with the responsibility of developing opportunities for the president to meet with students or creating environments that promote positive interactions between the president and students. The SSAO needs to know what the president thinks, wants, and expects when it comes to the area of student affairs. The president needs to be informed of campus activities or programs that allow passive engagement, as well as support in the development of intentionally designed focus groups that can provide him or her with an ongoing picture of student issues and concerns. Many presidents look to their SSAO as their conduit to the students. How well a SSAO accomplishes this task may shape this person's future.

In *Making a Difference: Profiles of Successful Student Affairs Leaders* (2001) Sandeen writes, "They all readily acknowledged that they served at the pleasure of their presidents, that they were on call 24 hours a day, 7 days a week, and that their futures could easily be determined by the way they responded (or failed to respond!) to a single issue" (p. 5).

This does not mean to imply that there is not room for disagreement or lively conversation with the president, but these dialogues should be done in private and in the appropriate forum. In the public forum, the president should always be secure in the knowledge that the SSAO is supporting the mission of the college and the focus of the presidency.

As young and midlevel professionals work in the field, one of the ongoing issues is that of moving into the SSAO role. Many questions arise concerning what path to take, whether there is a "right" path, and how current SSAOs made it to their position. I encourage all professionals to examine the book *Making a Difference* (Sandeen, 2001) as they ponder this question. Sandeen examines the lives of fifteen SSAOs who primarily worked at a single institution over the course of many years. In addition, he outlines the background of these professionals and the experiences that led them to their SSAO position. The stories of the leaders profiled in this book provide many different examples of successful routes to the SSAO position. Not surprisingly, being in the right place at the right time served many of these leaders well.

Conclusion

One might ask whether a title really matters. I maintain that it probably does not matter in terms of the work required in the position of SSAO. The vice president title may be a validation of the work that SSAOS have always done, or it may reflect the increasingly complex work required of small college institutional leaders in general. In any case, all of the work is important and contributes to the health of the institution and the experience of students on campus. The challenge, regardless of title, is doing it all as well as possible given changing demands and resources.

Brown (1997) reflected on the evolution of the senior student affairs officer's role on campus and discussed what he or she needs to know if the profession is to continue its evolution. Specifically, Brown wrote, "There is now a unique opportunity to take a proactive leadership role, to offer innovative programming that will improve not only campus life but also the total educational process. Chief student affairs officers can provide proactive leadership by viewing their positions as visionary, persuasive, and invaluable" (p. 546). Many SSAOs have seized this challenge and have become these individuals on their campuses. It is imperative that we continue to rise to meet the needs of our president and our colleges as we grow and expand as a profession.

References

Brown, C. L. "The Chief Student Affairs Officer and Leadership Effectiveness: Five Areas for Thought." *College Student Journal*, 1997, *31*, 545–551.

Palm, R. P. "Student Personnel Administration at the Small College." *NASPA Journal*, 1985, 22(3), 48–54.

Sandeen, A. *Making a Difference: Profiles of Successful Student Affairs Leaders.* Washington, D.C.: National Association of Student Personnel Administrators, 2001.

Tederman, J. S. *Advice from the Dean: A Personal Perspective on the Philosophy, Role and Approaches of a Dean at a Small, Private, Liberal Arts College.* Washington, D.C.: National Association of Student Personnel Administrators, 1997.

Walker, D. A., Reason, R. D., and Robinson, D. C. "Salary Predictors and Equity Issues for Student Affairs Administrators at Public and Private Institutions: From Dean to Director of Security." *NASPA Journal*, 2003, *40*(2), 134–152.

JANET HEETER BASS is vice president of student affairs and dean of students at Muskingum College in New Concord, Ohio.

NEW DIRECTIONS FOR STUDENT SERVICES • DOI: 10.1002/ss

5

The successful small college dean of students must develop and maintain an effective partnership between student and academic affairs, built on a shared educational philosophy, a mutual commitment to collaboration, and common linking issues and tasks.

Partners in a Community of Learners: Student and Academic Affairs at Small Colleges

Bruce W. Colwell

Until the early 1900s, the work of the contemporary senior student affairs officer (dean of students) and student affairs staff in American colleges was done entirely by the faculty or academic administrators, usually the president. By today's standards, nearly all colleges were small (fewer than five hundred students) and student life simple. Separate academic and student affairs, as we know them today, did not exist. Nineteenth-century American colleges were, in the English tradition, residential, undergraduate, liberal arts institutions, with a broad educational mission of intellectual instruction, moral (character) development, and preparation for vocation and citizenship. What we now view as student life was then seen as a part of a whole, single educational experience. Thus, even the title of this chapter, "Student *and* Academic Affairs," would have puzzled the early 1900s American college president.

Partnership and Collaboration

The primary thesis of this chapter is that the relationship between deans (the dean of the faculty or college, and the dean of students) and their academic affairs and student affairs divisions must be one of partners in a community of learners. This partnership means more than working as allies or occasional collaborators; they must be colleagues with shared values, goals, and language, committed to creating a single cohesive educational environment and experience for each student.

NEW DIRECTIONS FOR STUDENT SERVICES, no. 116, Winter 2006 © Wiley Periodicals, Inc.
Published online in Wiley InterScience (www.interscience.wiley.com) • DOI: 10.1002/ss.225

Kezar's national study of academic and student affairs collaboration (Kezar, 2001) identified four primary categories of reasons for significant academic and student affairs collaboration: (1) philosophical, with student learning as a shared institutional priority; (2) environmental, a collegial institutional environment with an ethos and tradition of collaboration; (3) managerial, the many tasks and linking issues addressed jointly; and (4) political, with institutional leadership advocating close student and academic affairs partnerships. This chapter examines the academic and student affairs relationship at small colleges from these four perspectives.

Throughout the twentieth century, academic affairs and student affairs developed separately. The dean of the faculty and the academic affairs staff narrowed its role within the institution to focus on student intellectual and academic development. The dean of students and student life staff worked almost exclusively with the nonacademic areas of the American college's broad educational mission: personal development, citizenship, and vocational preparation of students. Consequently, student and academic affairs are today two separate and distinct entities in most American colleges and universities. While the degree of separation and distinctiveness may be less at smaller institutions, this great divide is nonetheless a fundamental characteristic of the small college. At most small colleges, academic and cocurricular affairs are managed by separate administrative divisions, each led by a dean or senior officer with different educational and professional training. Each division has its own culture (Berquist, 1992), ethos, and professional language. Administratively, academic affairs and student affairs generally operate in separate institutional silos.

Yet student affairs professionals have resisted the growing separation between academic and student affairs. Today, early in the twenty-first century, a primary goal for many small college deans is to return student life to its historical position as an integral part at the core of the institution. This requires shifting from the view and language of twentieth-century student services, of support for the curricular and separate extracurricular activities, to again viewing those activities outside the classroom, particularly character development (ethics), personal growth, and vocational preparation, as an integral part of a college education, making academic and student life the two primary components of a single, whole educational experience.

Educational Philosophy: Why the Partnership Is Important

Student learning is the common philosophical ground for the academic and student affairs partnership. Student learning and development is the raison d'être of the small American college. For academic affairs, the centrality of student learning has always been clear and self-evident: all academic resources (classrooms, libraries) and activities (instruction) are about student learning. But for the American college student affairs professional, student learning has had a more peripheral place in the profession. This is

NEW DIRECTIONS FOR STUDENT SERVICES • DOI: 10.1002/ss

evident in the major philosophical statements issued by student affairs professional organizations over the past seventy years. The 1937 "Student Personnel Point of View" from the American Council on Education maintained that student affairs work supports and serves (hence, the commonly used professional descriptor, student *services*) students so they can fully engage in academic and intellectual learning. But the 1937 statement also challenged the narrower academic affairs definition of student learning by urging institutions to "consider the student as a whole. . . . [and emphasize] . . . the development of the student as a person rather than . . . intellectual training alone" (American Council on Education, 1937). Subsequent major statements—revisions of the "Student Personnel Point of View" in 1949 and 1983, "Student Learning Imperative" (American College Personnel Association (1996), and *Learning Reconsidered* (American College Personnel Association and National Association of Student Personnel Administrators, 2004) statements—emphasized that facilitating student learning (social, emotional, physical, spiritual, and vocational, as well as intellectual) outside the classroom was the primary purpose of student affairs rather than simply supporting the academic mission. Student affairs staff were therefore educators, the faculty for the nonacademic classroom. *Learning Reconsidered* went even further, arguing that all domains of student learning are interconnected and that all learning is interrelated and cannot be compartmentalized. With this understanding of student learning, the relationship of the faculty and academic affairs with student affairs staff is transformed from distant, occasional colleagues working with students in different areas to educational partners responsible for supporting all student learning.

The 1998 document *Powerful Partnerships: A Shared Responsibility for Learning* (itself a collaboration between a national academic affairs professional association and the two primary student affairs associations) "makes the case that only when everyone on campus—particularly academic affairs and student affairs staff—shares the responsibility for student learning will we be able to make significant progress in improving it" (American Association for Higher Education, American College Personnel Association, and National Association of Student Personnel Administrators, 1998, p. 1). The report defines the philosophical foundation of the academic and student affairs relationship with ten learning principles. "Learning is fundamentally about making and maintaining connections" (p. 3): among disciplines, ideas, and concepts; experientially between the mind and the environment; between deliberation and action; and through "classroom experiences integrated with purposeful activities outside of class" (p. 3). Furthermore, the report states, "Learning is enhanced by taking place in the context of a compelling situation that balances challenge and opportunity" (p. 3). These compelling situations occur in and outside the classroom, during and outside class time. Thus, they include the expectation of high standards of student behavior inside and outside the classroom (ethics and character development), giving students learning opportunities for leadership through

New Directions for Student Services • DOI: 10.1002/ss

internships, service-learning, study abroad, and workplace learning experiences. Each of the ten learning principles, the report contends, is applicable to learning both in and outside class, as well as to each of the learning domains. Thus, if academic and student affairs staffs have a common philosophical commitment to creating powerful learning environments on their campuses, it will be accomplished only with a strong working partnership.

This philosophical basis for a significant academic and student affairs partnership has particular importance in the small college, precisely because small college learning environments are so "developmentally powerful" (Hawley and Kuh, 1986, p. 11). Several of the learning principles operate more fully in the small college setting. The principle that learning occurs through interactions and opportunities for involvement suggests that the student at the less populated small campus, with a small student-faculty ratio and small class sizes, will have more frequent and more intense interactions, and consequently more learning. Principle 8, that "much learning *takes place informally and incidentally* . . . in casual contacts with faculty and staff" (American Association for Higher Education, American College Personnel Association, and National Association of Student Personnel Administrators, 1998, p. 8), finds fertile ground in the small college as "the power of the small college support system . . . lies in the greater accessibility and availability of responsible faculty and student affairs staff" (Hawley and Kuh, 1986, p. 17).

In addition, many American small colleges are primarily residential, with a liberal arts curriculum. As Kuh has argued convincingly, "The meta goal of student affairs, development of the 'whole person,' is consistent with the goals of general or liberal education" (Kuh and McAleenan, 1986, p. 110). Thus, at a small, residential, liberal arts college, academic and student affairs staff have a particularly rich common educational philosophy on which to build their partnership.

The Small College Environment: Collegial and Personal Communities

The relationship of academic and student affairs is shaped by the broader institutional environment, particularly the campus history and ethos regarding collaboration. One of the hallmark characteristics of a small college is its intensely personal and communal nature. As Kuh and McAleenan wrote in a seminal work, *Private Dreams, Shared Visions: Student Affairs Work in Small Colleges*, "At the core of every small college with a salient institutional purpose is a community of students, faculty, and staff with an emotional bond to the institution" (1986, p. 6). He argues that the particular ethos of the small college makes a close academic and student affairs relationship both more important and more likely.

Young (1986) asserts "that small school administration differs from large university administration" due to the presence of a "collective identity or ideology" (p. 71) at small schools. This distinctive small school ideology, he continues, is "characterized by more synergy, values education, personalized relationships, and organic change" (p. 71). At small schools, students, faculty, and staff are more likely to feel that they are part of an intimate personal community of learners that values people as whole individuals. For both academic and student affairs staff, this ethos supports close working relationships and encourages significant opportunity to participate together in the growth and learning of students.

This environment of personalism defines the role of the small college dean of students and student affairs staff; personalism is the "horse that student affairs personnel rode into small colleges" (Young, 1986, p. 74). Intense involvements with faculty and staff colleagues are almost inevitable. As Young notes, "It is not unusual for the small college chief student affairs officer to take coffee with or attend church with the football coach, the mathematician, the registrar, a psychology instructor, or the placement director" (Young, 1986, p. 74). And he might have added, "with the dean of the faculty."

The significance of personal relationships permeates the small college. The small college ensures human-scale learning environments, where the faculty and the dean of students have direct contact with nearly every student and know them by name. "The synergetic principle of student affairs practice in small colleges is student growth through contact with students" (Young, 1986, p. 73). Students select small colleges expecting to have significant personal relationships with other students, faculty, and staff; alumni from small schools identify peer friendships and relationships with faculty as the most valuable components of their educational experience.

The personal ethos on the small college campus requires student affairs staff to possess particular skills and play multiple roles. First and foremost, they must have exceptional communication and interpersonal skills. With personal interactions and relationships the primary means of working with students and staff, the successful dean of students must be an effective partner in myriad relationships. The roles include administrator and supervisor for staff and counselor, teacher, and disciplinarian with students. And with the dean of the faculty and academic affairs staff, the dean of students is variously consultant, advisor, facilitator, teammate, and always partner.

In this personal small college environment, the student affairs staff must be visible, accessible, and available not only to students but also to faculty and academic affairs staff. The credibility of student affairs staff with faculty is dependent on the frequency and quality of their interactions. At small schools, this relationship and its interactions may be strengthened by formal structures and roles, such as membership on the academic standing committee or the adjudicator of academic dishonesty cases. However, at the small college, the dean of students has the opportunity for informal interactions with many students' academic lives and will likely participate, for example, in the selection and awarding of student research awards or be

NEW DIRECTIONS FOR STUDENT SERVICES • DOI: 10.1002/ss

present at senior theses presentations. Similarly, faculty are able to interact with their students at plays, athletic events, and residential social activities.

Managerial and Administrative Tasks and Forms of the Partnership

Although the academic and student affairs partnership is strengthened by a shared educational philosophy and supported by the personal, collaborative ethos of the small college, it is most significantly shaped in working together on shared tasks and common linking issues. Both academic and student affairs staffs are increasingly challenged to "demonstrate program worth and quality, programmatic strengths and weaknesses, and contributions made to institutional mission and effectiveness" (Hirsch and Burack, 2001, p. 54). This accountability requires assessment of student learning, both cognitive/academic and affective. At the small college, the dean of students must convince the institutional research staff to include cocurricular learning in its institutional assessments, as well as participate directly in academic affairs research and key institutional assessment, including accreditation and long-range planning exercises. Retention, another common issue for both academic and student affairs, is particularly important at small, tuition-driven colleges. Research on student attrition indicates the importance of both informal student-faculty interactions (Tinto, 1987) and student involvement. Consequently, many small colleges have teams of student and academic affairs staff who monitor and support students at risk.

Information technology has transformed student learning. In the classroom, virtual discussions (the online caucus), PowerPoint presentations, and Web research define academic learning in the twenty-first century. Similarly, the student cocurricular residential experience is now fundamentally shaped by electronic communication (mail, instant messaging, and Facebook.com) and the computer-based entertainment of the CD, MP3, and DVD. Unfortunately, technology is also increasingly involved in student misconduct, such as academic dishonesty and electronic harassment. Information technology (IT), now central in most student curricular and cocurricular learning, is an increasingly important academic and student affairs linking issue. The senior academic and student life officers need to sit together on institutional IT advisory committees and together ensure that changing technologies are contributing positively to student living and learning on campus.

A final linking issue for academic and student affairs is the importance of understanding students and student learning. Academic pedagogy in American higher education has evolved over the past fifty years from a primary focus on teaching subject matter to facilitating student learning. This requires college instructors to understand their students and how they learn, and not simply have mastery of their disciplinary content. The small college dean and student affairs staff know the students well and know how their students learn; this is a primary purpose of student affairs work. Consequently, student life staff, particularly at small colleges, can be valuable consultants for faculty. This partnership brings student affairs knowledge of students and the student learning process together with faculty knowledge of course content.

These collaborations tend to take one of three forms (Kezar, 2001) on college campuses: as formal organizational structures, as curricular innovation and programmatic activities that support academic learning, and as cocurricular learning activities that involve faculty and academic affairs staff.

Organizational Structures. Not surprisingly, much of the most effective and meaningful academic and student affairs collaboration occurs within organizational structures. When academic and student affairs staffs work together in offices, centers, committees, and programs, a genuinely collaborative relationship develops. Even at small colleges, where collaboration may occur informally, the quality of the collaboration is usually enhanced by formal structures. The small college dean who is committed to a strong partnership with academic affairs will be well served by locating the most regular and important collaborations into these formal structures.

Learning Centers. Particularly at small colleges where teaching rather than research is the primary mission, faculty development centers emerged in the second half of the twentieth century to address student learning and pedagogy. These campus teaching-learning programs examine the process of learning and assist faculty with how they teach rather than what they teach; the focus is on the student, not the course content. Understanding students and how they learn has become a primary task of faculty development centers, which is also a central concern in student affairs work. The opportunity and potential for significant academic and student collaboration in these centers are self-evident.

However, at virtually all small colleges today, teaching and learning centers are located in academic affairs, staffed by faculty, and more focused on faculty teaching than student learning. Consequently, student affairs staffs typically participate in the centers only on advisory boards or as infrequent guest presenters on topics such as learning disabilities, disruptive students, and academic dishonesty. In the future, as these faculty development centers increasingly emphasize student learning and as student affairs expertise with students and student learning is recognized by the faculty, occasional and peripheral collaboration can grow into a true partnership. The faculty teaching and learning center of today could evolve into an institutional learning center, co-led by academic and student affairs, supporting student learning wherever it occurs, from the classroom and lab to the campus stages, playing fields, auditoriums, and residences. And it is at the small college, where teaching and student learning is singularly important and student learning beyond the classroom (civic engagement, ethics, citizenship and self-governance) is a valued and primary part of the institutional mission, that such an evolution is most likely.

Academic Progress Committees. Every campus has a committee to review and monitor student academic progress. These committees are, understandably, usually located in academic affairs and comprise the registrar, academic affairs staff, and faculty. Most institutions, recognizing the value of a student life perspective in these deliberations, include the dean of students or a designee. Even so, these committees are viewed primarily as academic, not institutional, structures. Like the learning centers, academic progress committees can be places for significant academic and student affairs partnership. At Carleton College, the student life class dean serves as the coordinator of the academic standing committee, and student affairs staffs (rather than academic affairs staff) have primary responsibility for monitoring academic progress during sessions, granting extensions, and adjudicating academic dishonesty cases. Administrative arrangements that regularly involve student affairs staff in the academic lives of students make visible the institutional philosophy that the entire college promotes student learning, both academic and cocurricular, in a single holistic student educational experience. Once again, it demonstrates that at small colleges, academic and student affairs work as genuine educational partners.

Academic Support Centers and Academic Advising. Academic support (study skills, tutoring, and supplemental instruction) and academic advising, areas closely related to classroom instruction but focused on student learning, use structures that vary among institutions. Historically, faculty handled both of these functions, and at most small colleges today, faculty continue to be the primary academic advisors. However, as both of these tasks address how students learn and require knowledge of the student, student affairs expertise is increasingly involved. Academic support centers typically provide study skill and time management assessment, tutoring, and support for students with learning disabilities; some include broad academic skill support for writing and math. Although many are staffed by faculty or former academics, increasingly graduates of student affairs programs are staffing these centers, and especially at small colleges the academic support centers are migrating to student affairs divisions.

Faculty continue to perform as academic advisors at most small colleges, and the advising system has remained in academic affairs. Particularly at small liberal arts colleges, where personal student-faculty relationships are especially valued, academic advising is seen as an extension of the faculty teaching role. Yet many faculty working outside their academic discipline feel less competent with individual advising interactions and understand this is what student affairs staff do well. Consequently, student affairs staffs are increasingly involved in the training (orientation sessions and workshops) and support of faculty advisors. Some larger institutions have created professionally staffed academic advising centers, but smaller institutions are both philosophically and financially committed to delivering academic advising through their faculty. Nevertheless, the key to an excellent advising program is divisional collaboration: "Constructing connections between academic affairs, student affairs, and support services can encourage students to become involved and to persist in college" (Frost, 1992, p. iv).

NEW DIRECTIONS FOR STUDENT SERVICES • DOI: 10.1002/ss

Institutional Committees. The academic and student affairs partnership is at work in a number of other structures at small colleges. Indeed, the small college commitment to providing a personal, whole, and cohesive educational experience for students encourages academic and student affairs collaboration virtually everywhere. There should be a student life voice on the education and curriculum committee, on the information technology advisory committee, and at the honors convocation. And just as certainly, there should be faculty membership on the student life committee, student judicial committees, and athletic advisory boards. Having significant committee membership from both divisions, rather than a single token representative, also demonstrates the strength of the partnership.

Interdivisional Partnership Structures. The ultimate expression of a significant academic and student affairs partnership may be in the creation of structures that reside between, and are equally a part of, each division. Even at the small college of the future, it seems likely that the complexities and challenges of both academic and student affairs will continue to require separate administrative entities. To best address some of the issues shared by both entities, new structures that transcend the boundaries of academic and student affairs may arise.

One such structure might be a center for experiential learning, combining in one office off-campus studies, academic service-learning, and ethical studies (usually in academic affairs) with career development and volunteer service programs (usually in student affairs). The Filene Center for Work and Learning at Wheaton College in Norton, Massachusetts, housed in academic affairs as the career center, takes a first step in this direction by defining itself as "the office that assists students in pursuit of meaningful out-of-classroom experiences." The Filene Center is part of the six-member Advising Collaborative Group, joining other academic affairs offices for academic advising, registration, global education, and collaborative learning with multicultural services from student affairs. Similarly, the center for experiential learning of the future would work with many types of out-of-class learning experiences, both academic and cocurricular. Such an administrative structure would be a full academic and student affairs partnership and might organizationally be located between the divisions.

Curricular Programmatic Activities. Service-learning, or academic civic engagement activities, in which out-of-class service experiences are incorporated into academic courses, is an area of growing academic and student affairs collaboration. Faculty found that they did not have the time or expertise to arrange off-campus learning experiences, yet this is precisely what student life staff were already doing in the college's extensive community volunteer programs. The partnership is a natural one and is likely to grow as more faculty bring service-learning into their courses. The challenge for student affairs may be providing adequate staff support to service-learning without compromising the quality of their extensive cocurricular volunteer programs.

NEW DIRECTIONS FOR STUDENT SERVICES • DOI: 10.1002/ss

Academic learning communities that "feature intentional groupings of students, coordinated scheduling, collaborative or cooperative learning techniques, and courses linked conceptually around common themes" (Kezar, 2001, p. 59) are often set in residential units (living–learning) where student affairs staff and faculty work together. Here, in- and out-of-classroom learning merges with increased faculty involvement in residential life. Other institutions have established student "cocurricular transcripts," formally acknowledging and sometimes granting academic credit for student service and leadership experiences. When this information is incorporated by faculty into academic and career advising, students benefit with more effective life planning.

Cocurricular Learning Activities. Extensive academic and student life collaboration also occurs with tasks and programs that are traditionally student life concerns. At most small colleges, significant collaboration is found in new student orientation and first-year-experience programs, life and career planning, leadership and service programs, and academic advising. The dean of students and staff must identify meaningful opportunities for faculty and other academic staff to participate in these student life programs. At small colleges, faculty are particularly interested in interactions with students outside the classroom, as they realize a fuller understanding of their students' lives can inform their classroom teaching. Faculty involvement and presence in these cocurricular programs also signal to students that these cocurricular activities are valuable (and valued by the institution) learning experiences.

Significant faculty and academic staff participation in new student and first-year-experience programs is critical. First and foremost, academic life is the center of the college experience, and therefore any authentic orientation or first-year program must involve academic staff. Second, the extent to which students see academic and student life staff working together shapes how they view faculty and student life staff and their learning: extensive collaboration suggests to students that both faculty and student life staff are educators and that their learning in and out of class is all part of a single, whole, educational experience. A common reading activity where all incoming students read the same book in the summer and during new student week participate in a convocation and small group discussion is a typical example of this collaboration. The discussion is facilitated by faculty, sometimes paired with a student life professional and a student leader. At a small school, the common reading groups can be kept to ten or fewer students and can thereby involve virtually all faculty and student life staff. These personal and powerful learning experiences are most likely at small schools with extensive academic and student staff collaboration.

Faculty are naturally involved in student career planning, especially for students headed to graduate school or taking credit internships. But a majority of students are not likely to have regular extensive career planning discussions with a faculty member. Most small colleges do not take advantage of the career advising potential of the major faculty advisor. However, some schools, like Wheaton College in Massachusetts, have made career planning an important part of their academic advising. Students write essays about their college and career expectations before enrolling, and advisors use this essay at each academic advising session over their four years. Wheaton's Filene Center prepares faculty to act as career counselors, and consequently the institution is ensured that all students are having regular and explicit career planning discussions throughout their enrollment. More typical of faculty involvement in career planning is Carleton College's departmental career coordinators, who work with the career center staff to arrange occasional talks by department alumni.

There can also be significant faculty involvement in other student affairs programs and activities. More faculty are adding a service component to their courses and often partnering with the student affairs volunteer services program to make arrangements with community sites. On campuses where the academic support centers are in student affairs, faculty are involved with the selection and training of student tutors, writing assistants, and course supplemental development assistants. Another collaborative service housed in student affairs at Carleton is provided by student departmental advisors, who are seniors selected by each department, trained by the dean of students staff, and who assist with a new-student-week academic fair, staff an annual majors fair, and provide peer academic planning advice.

Political Leadership: How Academic and Student Affairs Collaboration Happens

The dean of students and academic dean relationship at the small American college (and the student and academic affairs relationship) is shaped by institutional history, educational philosophy, the small college environment, and linking issues and common administrative tasks. But it is also a political relationship, defined by institutional position, power, and influence.

Historically, the dean of students position was part of the staff of the president or the dean of the faculty. Indeed, most early deans were faculty appointed to handle tasks such as student discipline, housing, extracurricular activities, and personal advising, for which the president, and then the dean of the faculty, simply had no time. Even today at some elite, selective small colleges, faculty are placed into senior student affairs positions. Everywhere, with the reality that academic affairs is the college's primary and central mission, the dean of students was inevitably in a politically subservient position. Consequently the dean of students at most small colleges either reports to the academic dean or more typically serves on the president's staff where the academic dean is "first among equals."

However, Kuh and others have noted that "small colleges are in desperate need of leadership from within," and "on a small campus, one person

NEW DIRECTIONS FOR STUDENT SERVICES • DOI: 10.1002/ss

with vision, compassion, energy, and good ideas cam make a difference" (Kuh and McAleenan, 1986, p. 109). At the small college, where the dean of students has significant interaction with many faculty and considerable access to the president, the dean has a genuine opportunity to provide institutional leadership and serve as an equally powerful and influential partner with the dean of the faculty and others who report directly to the president.

Class Dean Program at Carleton College

The class dean program instituted at Carleton College in 1996 is an example of a significant student and academic affairs partnership at a small college. Although many small colleges have class deans (that is, an identified student life professional who works with a given class, for example, the dean of freshman or the senior class dean), Carleton's class dean program is distinctive for the extent of the collaborative partnership. The class deans, Carleton faculty are reminded in a memo each fall, are "generalist advisors assisting students with academic information, personal advice, and referrals throughout their four years." Class deans are consultants for faculty, available to work with students who are having significant academic problems or exhibit health or emotional problems. The class dean role exemplifies Carleton's institutional belief that all student learning is connected and that academic and other learning (interpersonal, emotional, physical, vocational, and spiritual) are all important aspects of a Carleton education. This belief, a part of the history and ethos of many small residential liberal arts colleges, was manifest for decades in Carleton's associate dean for educational counseling position. The recent reorganization into class deans formalized the role that earlier associate deans had performed: they were the hub of the institutional advising wheel, the only advisor in a position to see the whole student and the whole educational environment.

The Carleton class dean position acknowledges that at the contemporary American college, even small colleges, faculty and staff have become specialists, working with a specific area of student learning and support. The institution is organized to work with separate parts of the student educational experience: faculty work with the student's intellect, coaches and health staff with the physical, the chaplain with the spirit, and career counselors with future vocation. The class dean position reclaims, at least partially, the generalist advisor role that faculty and presidents played in student lives a century ago. Thus, the Carleton class dean position is built on the small college historical tradition of development of the whole person and on the common philosophical foundation of academic and student affairs collaboration: student learning.

The position also grows from the small college ethos of personal interaction. The class dean at a small school can work directly with most students: by commencement, the Carleton class dean has typically met individually with more than 70 percent of a class. And for those students having the most difficulty, the class dean is often the only person with access to both academic and cocurricular information and the only consistent adult relationship throughout the student's college career. The educational impact of the class dean is made possible by and amplified at the small college. First, with a class of five hundred students, it is possible for a class dean to meaningfully work with 350 students (the 70 percent) over a four-year period. But perhaps more significant, the importance that both the institution and students at small schools place on personal encounters and individual interactions (the ethos of personalism) makes meaningful advising relationships more likely.

While institutional history, philosophy, and ethos provide a fertile soil for students to develop significant holistic advising relationships with the class dean, the relationships grow because the dean is working with students on significant academic and cocurricular tasks. The Carleton class deans are meaningfully involved in students' academic lives: processing all academic progress reports during terms and extensions (incompletes) after terms; as members of the academic standing committee, monitoring academic progress and work with students having difficulty; handling special majors and requests for exceptions to academic policies; organizing academic fairs and majors fairs; and training faculty advisors and student departmental advisors. In addition, class deans play the traditional student affairs role of working with individual students on any issue that affects their continuing enrollment: major health, personal, or disciplinary issues and processing status changes. As a result, student interactions with Carleton class deans are as likely to concern academic issues as cocurricular ones. Indeed, almost all conversations involve both, and through the class dean, a position that exemplifies the academic and student affairs partnership, Carleton students receive seamless educational advising.

The Future of the Academic and Student Affairs Partnership

The academic affairs and student affairs relationship is increasingly of primary importance for the small college dean. Philosophically, as student affairs continues to shift its emphasis from support and auxiliary service to student learning and development, the relationship will evolve from casual and distant administrative colleagues to one of significant educational partners. The gulf between the institutional silos will close as both divisions increasingly share common mission, language, and goals. The academic and student affairs partnership will be nourished by the collegial and personal ethos of the small college; the institution places significant value on meaningful individual interactions, between faculty and students both in and out of the classroom, between staff and students, and between academic and student affairs staff. Administratively, both divisions will have greater involvement in the other's primary issues and tasks, and new programs and structures will emerge between or on the borders of academic and student affairs. Politically, the small college dean of student affairs of the future, with an increasingly shared academic and student affairs mission and operation, will function with the dean of academic affairs as equal partners in a community of learning.

References

American Association for Higher Education, American College Personnel Association, and National Association of Student Personnel Administrators. *Powerful Partnerships: A Shared Responsibility for Learning: A Joint Report.* Washington, D.C.: American Association for Higher Education, American College Personnel Association, and National Association of Student Personnel Administrators, 1998.

American College Personnel Association. *The Student Learning Imperative: Implications for Student Affairs.* Washington, D.C.: American College Personnel Association, 1996. Retrieved May 2006 from www.myacpa/sli/sli.

American College Personnel Association and National Association of Student Personnel Administrators. *Learning Reconsidered: A Campus-Wide Focus on the Student Experience.* Washington, D.C.: American College Personnel Association and National Association of Student Personnel Administrators, 2004.

American Council on Education. Committee on Student Personnel Work. "The Student Personnel Point of View." 1937. Retrieved May 2006 from http://www.myacpa.org/pub/documents.

Berquist, W. H. *The Four Cultures of the Academy.* San Francisco: Jossey-Bass, 1992.

Frost, S. *Academic Advising for Student Success: A System of Shared Responsibility.* ASHE-ERIC Higher Education Report, no. 3. Washington, D.C.: George Washington University, School of Education and Human Development, 1992.

Hawley, K. T., and Kuh, G. D. "The Small College as a Developmentally Powerful Learning Environment." In G. D. Kuh and A.C. McAleenan (eds.)., *Private Dreams, Shared Visions: Student Affairs Work in Small Colleges.* Washington, D.C.: National Association of Student Personnel Administrators, 1986, 39–52.

Hirsch, D. J., and Burack, C. "Finding Points of Contact for Collaborative Work." In A. Kezar, D. J. Hirsch, and C. Burack (eds.). *Understanding the Role of Academic and Student Affairs Collaboration in Creating a Successful Learning Environment.* New Directions in Higher Education, no. 116. San Francisco: Jossey-Bass, 2001, 53–62.

Kezar, A. "Documenting the Landscape: Results of a National Study on Academic and Student Affairs Collaborations." In A. Kezar, D. J. Hirsch, and C. Burack (eds.). *Understanding the Role of Academic and Student Affairs Collaboration in Creating a Successful Learning Environment.* New Directions in Higher Education, no. 116. San Francisco: Jossey-Bass, 2001, 39–52.

Kuh, G. D., and McAleenan, A. C. (eds.). *Private Dreams, Shared Visions: Student Affairs Work in Small Colleges.* Washington, D.C.: National Association of Student Personnel Administrators, 1986.

Tinto, V. *Leaving College: Rethinking the Causes and Cures of Student Attrition.* Chicago: University of Chicago Press, 1987.

Young, R. B. "Notes on Student Affairs Administration in the Small College." In G. Kuh and A. C. McAleenan (eds.), *Private Dreams, Shared Visions: Student Affairs Work in Small Colleges.* Washington, D.C.: National Association of Student Personnel Administrators, 1986.

BRUCE W. COLWELL *is senior associate dean of students and a class dean at Carleton College in Northfield, Minnesota.*

This chapter provides a future-oriented look at what small college deans may encounter during the next decade while providing models for building and assessing a successful student life program.

The Future of the Small College Dean: Challenges and Opportunities

William J. Flanagan

> When you don't reach your own expectations, you make yourself vulnerable to the will of others.
>
> Tyrone Willingham, former head football coach,
> University of Notre Dame

What is the future of the small college dean? "Life will be interesting" might be the easiest—and flip—answer, especially for those of us who have been in this profession for any period of time. If the past twenty years are any indication of what the future might be, we know how dramatically campus life can change. We have experienced increasingly intrusive statutory and regulatory requirements such as the Family Educational Rights and Privacy Act and the Jeanne Clery Disclosure of Campus Security Policy and Campus Crime Statistics Act. We live and work in a more litigious environment than a decade ago. The emergence of "helicopter" parents is a major topic of discussion at conferences and professional meetings. Our campuses are experiencing increased numbers of students with diagnosed emotional and disability concerns. There has been a rapid expansion of technology, and it has had a subsequent impact on student life, both good and bad. Finally, one might argue that small colleges and universities like ours are being pushed toward a previous era when colleges acted in loco parentis.

I suspect many small college deans who value their interactions and relationships with students, recognize the power and value of their roles

New Directions for Student Services, no. 116, Winter 2006 © Wiley Periodicals, Inc.
Published online in Wiley InterScience (www.interscience.wiley.com) • DOI: 10.1002/ss.226

in the developmental process, and seek to create the very best living and learning environments possible for students may be asking such questions as: Will it be possible in the future to be the type of dean who is capable of knowing and working with students in positive and powerful ways during their developmental journey? Can I still be an effective dean of students despite the increased demands of the job, growing complexity of student life, and, for many, limited resources?

I strongly believe the answer to these questions is yes. Addressing increasingly complex student life issues in a manner consistent with the institution's mission and resources will require vision and leadership. The long-standing qualities of any effective dean will be necessary in the future: genuine concern and care for all students; being trustworthy and honest in all interactions with students, faculty, staff, and parents; awareness and understanding of the critical issues and concerns facing students; openness, candor, compassion, and ethical behavior; knowledge about how students grow, learn, and develop on college campuses; and a continuous desire to learn and change as times change.

The future of the small college dean will include three important realities. First, the increasingly complex nature of our profession will require substantial personal and professional preparation, experience, and ongoing professional development. Deans must be able to think critically, analytically, and from multiple perspectives. It will be increasingly important to develop essential competencies including research and assessment, interpersonal skills, oral and written communication skills, the ability to listen, and management and leadership skills. Second, senior student affairs officers (SSAOs) will be required to produce evidence that their division is accomplishing its learning goals and objectives. In short, assessment is here to stay. The third reality is that change is inevitable.

This chapter provides personal and professional insights that will, ideally, assist current and future deans of students at small colleges to explore some of the key challenges they will likely face during the next ten years. These challenges will exist whether they work at a resource-rich or resource-challenged institution. Models for building a comprehensive student life program and assessment plan are presented for consideration when confronting the challenges outlined in this chapter.

Background

Despite the challenges and changes facing our work over time, the two most anticipated days of the year for many of us continue to be opening day for new students and commencement. Each of these days has special significance for two important reasons. The first, and more obvious, reason is that they signal the beginning and end of our annual cycle. Opening day presents us and our staff with new opportunities, ideas, challenges, and faces. The day is upbeat, full of hope and promise—a new beginning for everyone.

NEW DIRECTIONS FOR STUDENT SERVICES • DOI: 10.1002/ss

Commencement is a time of closure, for saying our good-byes and, occasionally, good riddance. They are powerful and emotional days, frequently referred to as important rites of passage for students and their families, marking the transition from one stage of life to another.

But a second and perhaps more germane reason for our anticipation is the fact that these two days reflect the formal beginning and closure of our relationships with students. This is a critical period in their personal growth and development, when they are moving from late adolescence to early adulthood (Chickering and Reisser, 1993). It is, in fact, a period of time when students are the most interesting, challenging, engaging, and alive with promise, hopes, and dreams. As deans and members of the student affairs profession, we are fortunate to have the unique opportunity to play an important role, sometimes a prominent role, in this developmental process.

Each year on move-in day, I tell the parents of new students that leaving their son or daughter off at college is a very emotional day for them and their family. I also tell them that on commencement day, members of my staff and I may be just as emotional when the young men and women we have gotten to know so well during the past four years move on to new adventures. That is the reward for being dean of students at a small college, where the opportunity still exists for us to know and interact with many, if not most, of our students in ways that many of our colleagues at much larger institutions cannot.

A Rising Tide Lifts All Boats

As we begin to explore the future of the small college dean, one important point needs to be made. Senior student affairs officers will be the leaders on their campuses responsible for responding to changing student life issues in positive, active, productive, and educational ways. Student learning, including personal growth and development, is the primary reason our profession exists. When we truly understand and embrace the mission of our institution and work collaboratively with faculty and staff to improve the quality of student learning, other institutional goals will likely be affected in positive ways as well. For example, a positive living and learning environment enhances recruitment and retention efforts; collaboration and cooperation replaces the dreaded silo mentality; and the mission, learning goals, and advancement efforts of the college are more likely to be achieved. In short, a rising tide lifts all boats. This is the case whether our institutions have substantial resources or not.

The New Dean

It is interesting to note that many colleagues in recent years have been called on to provide leadership and management for areas that historically have reported to the president, provost, dean of the college, or other college officers. This change appears to be due to two primary factors. First, these college officers increasingly are being required to devote significantly more time and energy to advancing their institutions' curricular and fundraising initiatives, which are critical for the short- and long-term success of any small college. Second, presidents are more likely to turn to their SSAO for managing these new areas, as well as the traditional reports, when they are confident the professional in that role understands the big picture.

At the center of the big picture is an important but sometimes overlooked fact by some student affairs professionals: small colleges must have a well-defined educational mission that is attractive to students and their families. Students today, and in the future, will be far less likely to attend or graduate from colleges when they have concluded, correctly or incorrectly, that the academic program being offered cannot help them achieve their academic or career goals.

Sometimes one of the most challenging roles of the SSAO is to remind his or her staff, especially when resources are scarce, that the curriculum and academic offerings define the institution. For most students and families, the primary reason for selecting a particular college is their belief that the student's academic and career goals or interests can be satisfied through that institution's academic program. Equally important is determining if the investment is affordable or worthwhile. That said, when the academic and student life programs work in harmony with each other, student learning, growth, and development are enhanced whether students are in or out of the classroom. Everybody wins.

When the future suggests that small colleges will face shifting demographics, decreased support for higher education, and greater accountability, deans will have a special responsibility to build their staff and programs to support the institution's mission, student academic success, and student growth and development. By building a program that enhances and supports the college's mission and academic program, the SSAO will be viewed as a central team member in creating the type of living and learning environment that is crucial for any small college to attract and retain students. Once again, a rising tide lifts all boats.

Current and future college presidents must be certain that the institution's mission, curriculum, and faculty can deliver an academic program that is both attractive to students and worthy of the significant financial sacrifice they and their families must make when attending our colleges. Savvy presidents also understand that students and their parents expect much more from the colleges they attend. This attitude springs primarily from the published price of attending one of our colleges: tuition, room, board, and fees. But as we all know, the sticker price rarely covers the total cost of the education students receive at one of our colleges. Students and parents fully expect that in addition to a first-rate academic experience, colleges will provide attractive housing options, competitive financial aid packages, strong student advising, quality food service, well-appointed facilities, state-of-the-art technology, student support services for diagnosed disabilities, fun and engaging cocurricular programs and activities, competitive athletics, varied

NEW DIRECTIONS FOR STUDENT SERVICES • DOI: 10.1002/ss

recreational opportunities, and easily accessible counseling and health services, to name a few.

Effective presidents will provide the leadership in setting institutional
priorities and allocating scarce resources. But presidents will rely heavily on
their SSAO to help achieve the appropriate balance necessary for recruiting
and retaining students. For that reason, it is important for future deans to
build and assess their student life programs with the institution's mission as
the guiding principle, a solid theoretical base for training and assessment purposes, regular analysis of real data (not anecdotal information), and hiring
the best staff who truly value the small college experience. By approach-
ing the challenges at hand with these components in place, the SSAO will be
in a strong position to make the case for how the student life program complements the institution's mission, academic program, and learning goals.

There are several areas where small college presidents may rely on their
SSAO to support the academic mission of the college while providing a comprehensive and collaborative approach to the out-of-classroom learning
environment: admissions and financial aid, athletics, disability services, federally funded programs (such as Upward Bound, Student Support Services,
and McNair Scholars programs), academic advising (especially those that
incorporate a developmental advising philosophy), multicultural programs,
religious and spiritual life programs, experiential learning programs, and
community outreach and volunteer programs. Each of these areas offers
unique opportunities to build a comprehensive and coordinated cocurricular program that offers students valuable learning opportunities that occur
outside the classroom.

Building a Foundation for the Student Affairs Division and Retention

For many small colleges, the issue of student recruitment and retention is
the top institutional priority. Vincent Tinto's theory of student engagement
(1987) provides a solid foundation for current and future deans to build
their institution's student life program. Understanding that student commitment to an institution occurs over time, the model shown in Figure 6.1 outlines a potential structure for SSAOs to consider when building a
comprehensive student life program. This model takes into consideration
three key principles. First, the academic and social integration of students
takes time, perhaps up to two or more years for some students. Second, the
preentry attributes, needs, and challenges of students must be understood
and considered when developing programs, policies, and strategies to
address them, especially during the first two years. Third, as students grow,
develop, and move toward graduation, what they need or desire from the
institution will change as well.

Deans who are building student life programs must begin with the
mission and learning goals of the institution. Student life programs not in

Figure 6.1. Student Life and Retention Model

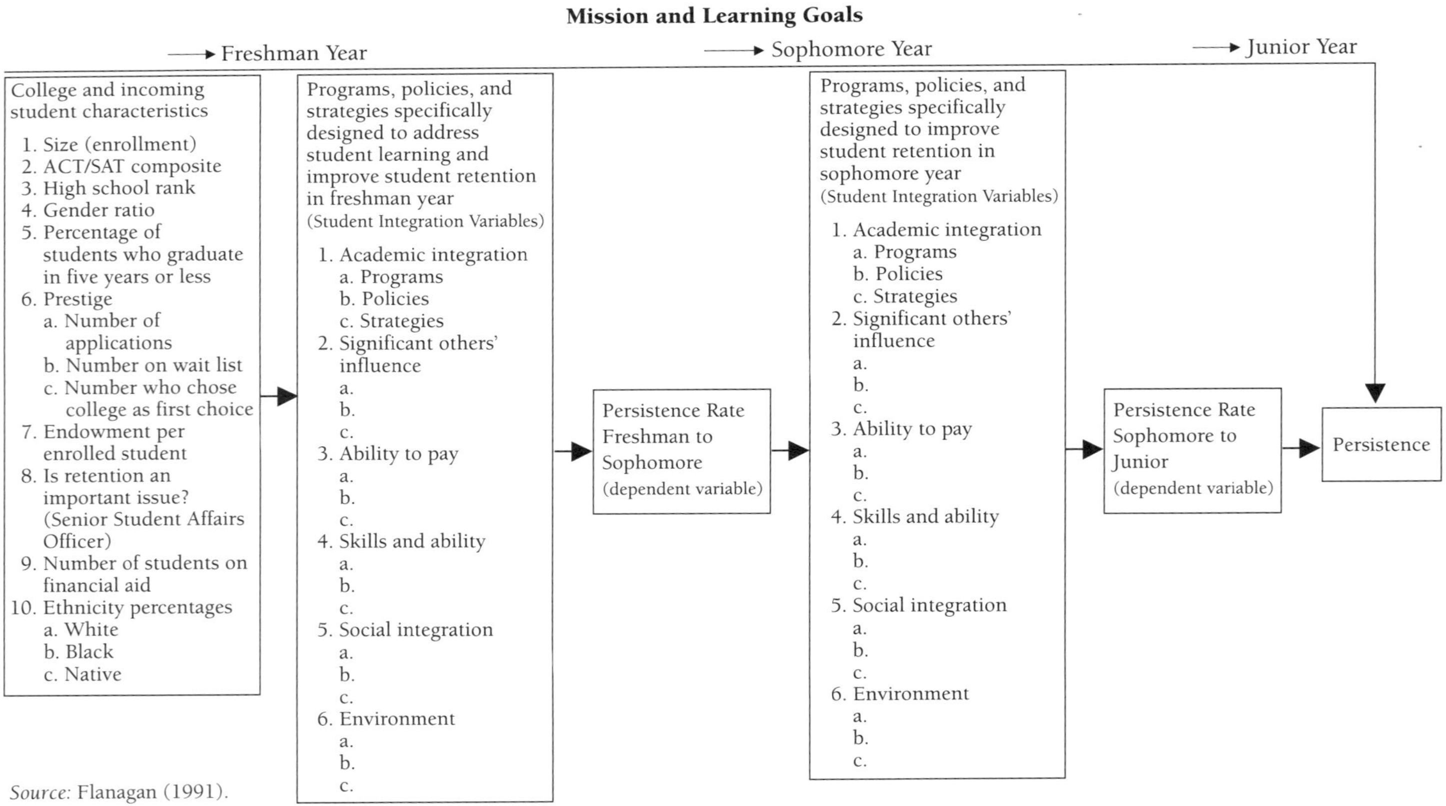

Mission and Learning Goals

→ Freshman Year → Sophomore Year → Junior Year

College and incoming student characteristics

1. Size (enrollment)
2. ACT/SAT composite
3. High school rank
4. Gender ratio
5. Percentage of students who graduate in five years or less
6. Prestige
   a. Number of applications
   b. Number on wait list
   c. Number who chose college as first choice
7. Endowment per enrolled student
8. Is retention an important issue? (Senior Student Affairs Officer)
9. Number of students on financial aid
10. Ethnicity percentages
    a. White
    b. Black
    c. Native

Programs, policies, and strategies specifically designed to address student learning and improve student retention in freshman year (Student Integration Variables)

1. Academic integration
   a. Programs
   b. Policies
   c. Strategies
2. Significant others' influence
   a.
   b.
   c.
3. Ability to pay
   a.
   b.
   c.
4. Skills and ability
   a.
   b.
   c.
5. Social integration
   a.
   b.
   c.
6. Environment
   a.
   b.
   c.

Persistence Rate Freshman to Sophomore (dependent variable)

Programs, policies, and strategies specifically designed to improve student retention in sophomore year (Student Integration Variables)

1. Academic integration
   a. Programs
   b. Policies
   c. Strategies
2. Significant others' influence
   a.
   b.
   c.
3. Ability to pay
   a.
   b.
   c.
4. Skills and ability
   a.
   b.
   c.
5. Social integration
   a.
   b.
   c.
6. Environment
   a.
   b.
   c.

Persistence Rate Sophomore to Junior (dependent variable)

Persistence

Source: Flanagan (1991).

harmony with the mission and values of the institution develop problems very quickly. In addition, the division of student affairs must understand what kind of students are attending and graduating from their institutions. Knowing this information makes it possible to tailor the programs, resources, and services to meet student needs. This understanding can come only from an assessment program where data are collected, analyzed, and fed back into the planning and decision-making processes. Important data might come from the admissions office, survey information such as the Cooperative Institutional Research Program survey that many colleges and universities use, and other data collected by the institution. For example, if the trend of incoming classes suggests that a substantial percentage of the students are first-generation, low-income students from disadvantaged backgrounds or with diagnosed learning disabilities, then developing learning centers, tutorial programs, and other appropriate support systems will be necessary.

SSAOs understand that one important measure of institutional success for which they are frequently held accountable is student persistence to graduation, typically measured by four- and six-year rates. As Tinto's theory (1987) and the model in Figure 6.1 demonstrate, students who feel connected to the institution both academically and socially are more likely to graduate. This is the principal reason that the partnership and collaboration between academic and student affairs is essential: students who select a college because the academic program fulfills their intellectual and career goals and interests (academic integration) and find satisfying friendships, out-of-class experiences, and services (social integration), are more likely to persist to graduation (Tinto, 1987; Flanagan, 1991). The relationship of academic and social integration, so vital in the student persistence model, is also a factor in why presidents and provosts turn to student affairs professionals to create and manage the living and learning environments that support the institution's mission and learning goals. As competition between colleges and universities intensifies during the next ten years, colleges that manage this relationship effectively will have a strong recruitment and retention advantage over those that do not.

Deans and other key administrators must also be sensitive to several additional factors that may affect student persistence to graduation. For example, in Figure 6.1, students may be satisfied with their academic program and have many friends and cocurricular commitments, but feel the cost is too burdensome (ability to pay). Ensuring that students experience ample opportunities to interact with supportive adult role models (faculty and staff) is important (significant others' influence). Providing appropriate and time-sensitive assistance and support to students whose academic or personal skills and abilities need improvement is vital (skills and ability). This is especially true if the institution admits a significant percentage of at-risk students. Finally, assessing the internal and external environment of the campus for the kinds of services, recreational offerings, and support systems that students need is an important component of this model. Student satisfaction with the internal and external environment will shape their undergraduate experience and decision making (environment) (Flanagan, 1991).

Developing a model for student life programs enables the SSAO to plan and assess progress more effectively. It is especially helpful in educating internal and external constituencies about how and why the division of student affairs does what it does. Most important, a model like Tinto's or the one in Figure 6.1 clearly demonstrates that student growth and development occur over time: what students need early in their college experience is different from what they need in their sophomore, junior, or senior years. Preparing and planning for these different needs will ensure the student life program is designed around the learning needs of students. Such an approach will be vital for an increasingly competitive environment.

Issues and Challenges for the Small College Dean

A number of issues and challenges that we explore in this section are likely to confront deans during the next seven to ten years: student body diversity; the changing campus environment, including the increasing role of parents, demands for amenities and services, and generational differences; students with diagnosed learning and emotional disabilities; interinstitutional competition; technology; and assessment.

Student Body Diversity. Perhaps the most challenging issue confronting many small college deans will be the need for their institutions to create more welcoming living and learning environments for an increasingly diverse student population. Demographic trends suggest that among traditional-aged college students, there will be a decrease in the percentage of white students and a significant increase in the percentage of students of color (Dennis, 2005). Small college deans will be at the center of institutional planning and response when creating the recruitment and retention efforts necessary for their institutions to adapt to this demographic shift.

One outcome of the recent U.S. Supreme Court case involving the University of Michigan's Law School admissions process, designed to increase ethnic diversity, is the Court's finding that a diverse campus community is a legitimate institutional goal for improving student learning experiences (*Grutter* v. *Bollinger,* 2003). This finding, coupled with current and future demographic trends, suggests that institutions would be wise to create campus learning environments that are more reflective of our increasingly diverse American society. Consequently, the skills and insights that deans of students should possess will be called on as colleges develop recruitment and retention efforts designed to increase campus diversity. Diversity should not be limited simply to ethnic diversity. We can expect campus diversity will be broadened to include socioeconomic, cultural, geographical, international, and, in many instances, gender diversity. Finally, many colleagues have reported increasing gaps in the gender ratio on their campuses. For many small colleges, recruiting and retaining traditional-aged male students is a growing challenge (Hodges, 2005).

Dennis (2005) provides an excellent analysis of significant trends in American higher education. For example, she reports that based on information obtained from the National Center for Education Statistics' "Projections of Education Statistics to 2011" (p. 12), we can expect these trends:

By 2012, higher education enrollments will total nearly 18 million.
Private institution enrollment will jump by 16 percent to 4.1 million students (public institutions will increase by 15 percent to 13.5 million students).
Male and female enrollments will increase: females to 10.3 million from 8.7 million and males from 6.6 million to 7.5 million.

She also predicts the following trends:

Women, minorities, and adult learners will dominate higher education enrollments.
College administrators will focus less on entrance information and more on exit assessment, competency-based degrees, retention and graduation, graduate school acceptance, career placement, and alumni satisfaction.
Traditional colleges and universities will not disappear, but they will change organizationally and will be managed differently in the future.

As an example of how diversity is changing and will continue to change for the next seven years, consider the following trends that Dennis predicts:

About 65 percent of the projected growth in population through 2020 will be in ethnic minority groups. The Hispanic population will increase by 34.7 percent, Asian by 33.3 percent, black by 12.9 percent, and white by 2.8 percent.
According to the American Council on Education, the number of minority high school graduates between the ages of eighteen and twenty-four enrolled in colleges and universities more than doubled to 4.3 million in the two decades that ended in 2000–2001. However, the college participation rate for African Americans was 40 percent and for Hispanics 34 percent.
Students of color will represent 80 percent of the increase in college-age students over the next decade.

What Dennis's research and current studies on demographic shifts make clear is that the traditional-aged population of students attending small colleges is changing significantly and will continue to change for the next decade. Being able to afford higher education will be a continuing challenge for students and families; small institutions will also face significant challenges when recruiting, retaining, and providing the support necessary

NEW DIRECTIONS FOR STUDENT SERVICES • DOI: 10.1002/ss

for the diversification of our campus communities. Consequently, the significant question that we in small colleges need to consider is: How will we recruit, engage, retain, support, and graduate this changing student demographic? This is an extremely important question for all college administrators, not just the dean, to consider when developing long-range and strategic goals.

Many of our students arrive on campus assuming it will be a diverse living and learning environment, since they come from high schools that are ethnically and culturally diverse. Diversity is an expectation. *Grutter* v. *Bollinger* established that campus diversity is recognized as a legitimate and important component of the educational environment for student learning. Both of these factors point to the importance of SSAOs being proactive in promoting and creating positive and supportive living and learning environments for a diverse community of students. Recruiting and retaining a diverse campus community—students, faculty, and staff—will be challenging for many of our institutions. Perhaps no other challenge has the potential to improve the quality of our learning environments while increasing the likelihood of achieving enrollment objectives.

Finally, to ensure that campuses are making efforts to achieve greater diversity, accrediting organizations like the Higher Learning Commission of the North Central Association require institutions to include statements on diversity in their mission statements and self-study documents. For example, the Higher Learning Commission's first criterion for accreditation is, "In its mission documents, the organization recognizes the diversity of its learners, other constituencies, and the greater society it serves" (2003, p. 3.2–2). There is an expectation that colleges and universities are making concerted efforts to diversify their student bodies, faculties, and staff to ensure students are exposed to, learn from, and are challenged by people, ideas, cultures, and values different from their own.

Parents, Demands, and Generational Differences. Julie Lythcott-Haims, dean of freshman and transfer students at Stanford University, writes: "'Helicopter parents'—the growing population of parents who hover a mere cell phone call away from resolving any need or concern in the lives of their increasingly complicit college age children—were once a confounding oddity but now seem to be a mainstay on the American landscape" (2005, p. 1). The situation has progressed to the point that colleges are beginning to set limits on the roles parents play in the lives of their children. Colgate University in upstate New York may be the most visible example. Prior to the start of classes in fall 2005, Colgate sent a letter to parents encouraging them to think about the undergraduate experience as "teachable moment" opportunities. Adam Weinberg, dean of the college, encourages parents to let students work out their problems rather than "hover" over them. "We noticed what everybody else noticed. We have a generation of parents that are heavily involved in their students' lives and it causes all sorts of problems. . . . College should be a time when you go from living in someone else's house

NEW DIRECTIONS FOR STUDENT SERVICES • DOI: 10.1002/ss

to becoming a functioning, autonomous person" (Colgate University, 2005, n.p.). Educating parents about the importance of letting go will be critically important for student affairs professionals and challenging as well. Achieving independence and personal and emotional autonomy is vital for students moving from late adolescence to early adulthood (Chickering and Reisser, 1993).

If personal experience is any indication of what other deans are finding on their campuses, contacts by parents on virtually any issue or concern is significantly higher in recent years than at any other time in memory. Campus life issues such as roommate conflicts, discipline, course registration, academic progress, health questions, and food preparation, to name just a few, frequently involve parents. In many instances, parents intervene for their son or daughter before the student has made any attempt to address the problem. Staff members in other areas report similar encounters.

By all accounts, this trend will continue. What is ironic about this situation is that the parents who are most involved in the lives of their children, the baby boomers, are the generation who brought to an end the concept of in loco parentis during the 1960s and 1970s. Lythcott-Haims (2005) comments: "Regardless of whether love or guilt drives it [their involvement], I wonder whether these Boomers realize that they are depriving the children they love so much of learning to do for themselves? And that this is nothing short of devastating, because implicit in our intergenerational compact is the presumption that parents must teach children to fend for themselves?" (n.p.).

Small college deans who are the campus's student development specialists and educators will be called on to navigate these potentially rocky waters. (For an in-depth analysis and suggestions for best practices, see Keppler, Mullendore, and Carey, 2005.)

Students and parents also are having an impact on other significant changes in campus culture, including how and why resource allocations are being made. As an example, students and parents fully expect that a wide range of up-to-date facilities, outstanding faculty and staff, services, programs, and amenities will be available when they enroll at a particular college. These expectations have created intense pressure for colleges to increase enrollments, commit to potentially dangerous long-term debt, and engage in intense interinstitutional competition for students. Unfortunately, this competition will result in some colleges losing sight of their missions while mortgaging their future. This trend may especially have an impact on those institutions that rely almost exclusively on student enrollment for survival. I fear that some, if not many, of these institutions will not survive, especially as the current demographic boom begins to recede in the next seven to ten years.

Fain (2005) explores in depth the arguments for expanding enrollments to address the competition and pressures facing small colleges. Douglas Bennett, president of Earlham College, states, "The upward pressure for size has an intellectual push, it has market push . . . and if you're committed to being small, you just have to wake up every morning and say, How do we resist those pressures? . . . . The quest for more—bigger operating budgets, more facilities, higher enrollment can be linked to academe's shift toward an increasingly corporate, numbers-heavy approach. And enrollment and campus growth are among the top achievements by which governing boards, alumni, and donors measure college presidents" (p. 26A). Deans will feel the effects of consistent growth, especially if housing, staffing, and programs are not increased at a rate consistent with this growth. When enrollment increases without consideration to the impact it will have on the campus overall, student satisfaction and campus morale can be negatively affected.

Adding to the pressure for institutional competition are the magazines and college guides that rank colleges and universities. *U.S. News and World Report*'s list of what it refers to as "America's Best Colleges" may be the most dramatic example. These rating systems send powerful messages to internal and external constituencies about what counts in terms of quality. Consequently, that this heightened competition among institutions has created significant problems for small colleges, especially those with limited resources, should come as no surprise. Although Earlham has made the decision to resist growth, at least for now, many small colleges may not be in the position to do so. Deans must be in partnership with other campus leaders in determining what is best for their institution. When resources are scarce, these discussions and decisions are complex and difficult. Ultimately the deciding factor must be what is best for the institution.

Students with Diagnosed Learning and Emotional Disabilities. One issue that has had a significant impact on small colleges is the increasing number of students with diagnosed learning disabilities and mental health diagnoses. This issue is one of the most challenging facing small college deans today and is not likely to go away. With growing frequency, articles, books, and consultants are detailing what should, or should not, be done by practitioners to address the problem. What is a dean supposed to do? Add staff, outsource counseling and disability services, keep an attorney on retainer, ignore the problem and hope it goes away? On any given day, each or all of these options may seem like a good approach.

The Elizabeth Shin case, in which a student at the Massachusetts Institute of Technology committed suicide on campus, garnered national attention when her parents successfully sued the institution. Part of their claim was that the institute, including student affairs officers, had abrogated its responsibility for the health and well-being of their daughter. Although the case was ultimately settled out of court, many deans across the country are coming to terms with the thought that their institutions can be sued for student behavior related to mental health issues. Small college deans, with considerably fewer mental health resources than larger counterparts and perhaps a more welcoming and supportive environment for students with a history of mental or emotional illness, may find themselves in particularly precarious positions.

A *Wall Street Journal* editorial noted, "Caught in a double-bind after an era when privacy and autonomy concerns ruled, colleges can safely respond to the modern understanding of *in loco parentis* only by spending more for legal advice and intensified counseling programs. Parents who complain about higher tuition bills—or missing report cards—are the least of an administrator's worries these days" ("In Loco Parentis Goes Loco," 2005, p. W13).

Interinstitutional Competition. Selingo (2005) describes the financial issues facing Bates College in Lewiston, Maine. Most of us can identify with Bates and the problems institutional leaders there face: attracting a diverse student body; keeping the education they offer affordable; managing escalating fixed costs like fuel, health insurance, utilities, and salaries; and providing facilities and programs that are comparable to those of their competition. Bates and many similar institutions, some richer and many poorer, are facing the same dilemma.

Although these issues affect the entire institution, deans are placed in the delicate situation where they must advocate for critically important facilities and programs. Residence halls, campus centers, and athletic and fitness facilities, for example, carry significant price tags. There are arguments to be made both for and against building projects or programs that center on the institution's ability to recruit and retain students. This is where the dean must be prepared with factual information about why a particular project is important for its impact on undergraduate learning, as well as its recruitment and retention potential. A well-developed assessment plan is instrumental in helping an institution set priorities. Student satisfaction surveys that gather data from students who matriculate, as well as those who do not, can be invaluable when setting priorities. Exit interviews and focus groups are also valuable sources of information about student attitudes.

SSAOs must be cognizant of potential institutional liability if projects are not undertaken. For example, knowing if residence halls meet local or state building codes or athletic facilities are comparable for men and women can be critically important when deciding on a course of action. In some cases, the decision for needing to comply with an unfunded mandate may be compelled by external decision makers such as state or local officials. Examples might include campus accessibility for the handicapped, the installation of sprinkler systems in residence halls, or the addition of parking spaces to meet local codes. Being aware of the law and externally mandated compliance issues will make it possible for the SSAO to influence the establishment of intuitional priorities. Ultimately all decisions rest on the resources available. Having the data to support a particular course of action is extremely important for any SSAO now and in the future.

Nevertheless, a simple fact remains: students and parents will select an institution based on factors difficult to quantify. Deciding where to invest scarce dollars to attract and retain students is challenging. I can recall talking to one student who chose our college because he thought it was "cool" we served hot dogs the day he and his family visited our campus.

NEW DIRECTIONS FOR STUDENT SERVICES • DOI: 10.1002/ss

Technology. One significant change in student and campus life is the growth of technology. Technology in many different forms is ubiquitous on campuses today and expected to grow even more in the future. One need only walk through the residence halls on opening day to see the number of students bringing their own computers to campus. But students also bring their MP3 players, cell phones, video game consoles, games, and other technology-related paraphernalia. Smart classrooms and advanced computer labs are important to them and their learning. In many ways, technology is wonderful for students and campuses. What would we do without e-mail? New technological innovations are providing unique opportunities for student learning, communications, and access to vast amounts of information.

Unfortunately there are potentially serious problems related to technology and how it can be used on campuses. Examples of technology used inappropriately by students include, but are not limited to, plagiarism, assignments bought or downloaded from the Internet, changing grades by hacking into the college's administrative software, cell phone cheating, and electronic harassment. Compounding the potential problems for campus life are Web sites like facebook.com, myspace.com, and myprofessors.com, to name just three sites that students use or visit extensively.

What makes this an important issue for SSAOs is the potential for personal or physical harm and poor decision making by students. Information and pictures placed on these and similar Web sites have been used in ways unintended by the students who frequent the sites. Instances of stalking, harassment, libel, illegal activities, and loss of job opportunities have all been reported in the popular press, on campuses, and in the courts. Technology is evolving every day and requires that SSAOs be attuned to the potential opportunities and challenges it brings to campus.

Assessment. The final critical issue addressed here is assessment. Federal and state governments and accrediting agencies increasingly are asking colleges and universities a fundamental question: "Can you provide evidence that students are learning what you say they will learn at your institution?" Put in simpler terms, "Are you doing what you say you are doing?" Answering that question is only part of the assessment process. Establishing learning goals and objectives based on the institution's mission statement, collecting appropriate data, and feeding the results of those data back into the planning and decision-making process are critically important components of a comprehensive and successful assessment process.

Many institutions and student life programs have developed curricular and cocurricular goals for student learning. Furthermore, many regularly collect significant amounts of quantitative and qualitative data that may address the learning goals in question. In many instances, based on my years of experience as a consultant and evaluator for the North Central Association's Higher Learning Commission, institutions fail to develop instruments or collect data that help determine if the learning goals have been met, or they may fail to feed data analysis back into the planning and decision mak-

Figure 6.2. Assessment Cycle

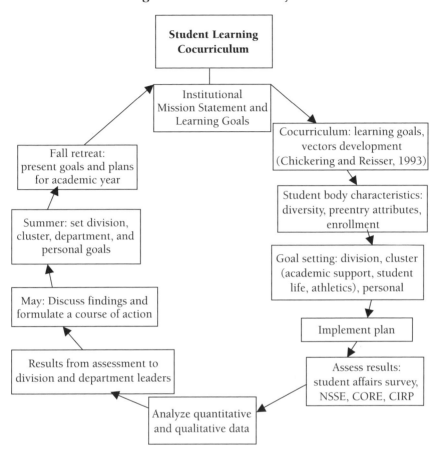

ing process. Figure 6.2 presents an assessment model highlighting the centrality of the institutional mission statement in developing cocurricular learning goals. The model emphasizes the yearly cycle of feeding the collected and analyzed data into the planning and decision making processes.

Chickering and Reisser's theory of student development (Chickering and Reisser, 1993), a standard in graduate preparation programs, is the basis for this model of a cocurriculum, learning goals, and assessment cycle. Other theories and approaches are certainly possible, although deans might consider building their cocurriculum and student learning goals on a well-established and thoroughly researched theory. Doing so offers two important advantages: comparison data with other programs and benchmarking capabilities. In Figure 6.2, the learning goals of the cocurriculum will enable students to:

NEW DIRECTIONS FOR STUDENT SERVICES • DOI: 10.1002/ss

Develop a sense of purpose where they are able to formulate personal, intellectual, and career goals.

Develop competence and experience growth in their intellectual, interpersonal, and physical skills through achievements and interactions with the curriculum and cocurriculum.

Learn to manage their emotions in order to balance self-expression with responsible actions.

Move through autonomy toward interdependence through interactions and exposure to those different from themselves and by increasing their capacity for intimacy and empathy and developing respect for human differences.

Develop their personal identity by becoming aware of their gender, sexual orientation, self-acceptance, and self-esteem.

Develop integrity by learning that personal responsibility and integrity are the essential qualities necessary for life, work, and community living.

Data obtained from nationally developed surveys such as the National Survey of Student Engagement, Cooperative Institutional Research Program, Core Institute Drug and Alcohol Survey, and the American Council of Education surveys administered during the sophomore and senior years provide ample evidence of student learning over the course of the undergraduate experience. Institutions should supplement these data with locally designed instruments to measure student learning and satisfaction. Focus groups, exit interviews, and department-specific assessment tools provide valuable data that ensure that planning and decision making are based on factual information, not anecdotal perceptions. When this approach is taken, progress can be made in terms of student learning, allocation of resources, and educating the campus community about the importance of student affairs in achieving the institution's mission and learning goals.

Conclusion

SSAOs will continue to play an important role in the lives of students and their institutions in the years ahead. As our profession has amply demonstrated over time, challenges and opportunities will abound. In the final analysis, SSAOs at small colleges and universities will influence the learning experiences of students at their institutions whatever their mission and resources happen to be. This is, and always has been, a tremendous responsibility.

Our profession will continue to evolve as times change and students change. Nevertheless, the fundamental principles that guided our professional roles in the past will continue to guide us in the future. And the cycle of welcoming and commencement ceremonies will continue to serve as annual reminders of why we do what we do: student learning, growth, and development.

NEW DIRECTIONS FOR STUDENT SERVICES • DOI: 10.1002/ss

References

Chickering, A. W., and Reisser, L. *Education and Identity.* (2nd ed.) San Francisco: Jossey-Bass, 1993.

Colgate University. "Partnering for a Colgate Education." Sept. 2, 2005. Retrieved Jan. 23, 2006, from http://www.colgate.edu/parents.

Dennis, M. J. *Ten Trends in Higher Education.* Madison, Wis.: Magna Publications, 2005.

Fain, P. "Is Less More at Small Colleges?" *Chronicle of Higher Education,* Sept. 9, 2005, p. A26.

Flanagan, W. J. "Sophomore Retention: The Missing Strategy in Small College Retention Efforts." Unpublished doctoral dissertation, University of Wisconsin-Madison, 1991.

Grutter v. Bollinger. 539 U.S. 306 (2003). Retrieved Jan. 23, 2006, from http://supct.law.cornell.edu/supct/html/02–241.ZO.html.

Higher Learning Commission. *Handbook of Accreditation: The Higher Learning Commission.* (3rd ed.) Chicago: Higher Learning Commission, 2003.

Hodges, M. H. "Where Are the Boys?" *Detroit News,* Dec. 4, 2005. Retrieved Dec. 6, 2005, from http://www.detnews.com/apps/pbcs.dll/article.

"In Loco Parentis Goes Loco." *Wall Street Journal,* Sept. 23, 2005, p. W13. Retrieved Sept. 26, 2005, from http://online.wsj.com/article/0,,SB112744003984149535,00.html.

Keppler, K., Mullendore, R. H., and Carey, A. (eds.). *Partnering with the Parents of Today's College Students.* Washington, D.C.: National Association of Student Personnel Administrators, 2005.

Lythcott-Haims, J. "When Did Caring Become Control? Blame Boomers." *Chicago Tribune,* Oct. 16, 2005, sec. 2, pp. 1, 7.

Selingo, J. "How Much Is Too Much?" *Chronicle of Higher Education,* Oct. 21, 2005, p. A30.

Tinto, V. *Leaving College: Rethinking the Causes and Cures of Student Attrition.* Chicago: University of Chicago Press, 1987.

WILLIAM J. FLANAGAN is vice president for student affairs and dean of students at Beloit College in Beloit, Wisconsin.

NEW DIRECTIONS FOR STUDENT SERVICES • DOI: 10.1002/ss

INDEX

Back Issue/Subscription Order Form

Copy or detach and send to:
Jossey-Bass, A Wiley Imprint, 989 Market Street, San Francisco CA, 94103-1741

Call or fax toll-free: Phone 888-378-2537 6:30AM – 3PM PST; Fax 888-481-2665

Back Issues: Please send me the following issues at $28 each
(Important: please include ISBN number for each issue.)

_____

_____

_____

$ _____   Total for single issues

$ _____   SHIPPING CHARGES: SURFACE   Domestic Canadian

		First Item	$5.00	$6.00
		Each Add'l Item	$3.00	$1.50

For next-day and second-day delivery rates, call the number listed above.

Subscriptions   Please __ start __ renew my subscription to *New Directions for Student Services* for the year 2_____at the following rate:

U.S.	__ Individual $80	__ Institutional $195
Canada	__ Individual $80	__ Institutional $235
All Others	__ Individual $104	__ Institutional $269

**For more information about online subscriptions visit
www.wileyinterscience.com**

$ _____   Total single issues and subscriptions (Add appropriate sales tax for your state for single issue orders. No sales tax for U.S. subscriptions. Canadian residents, add GST for subscriptions and single issues.)

__Payment enclosed (U.S. check or money order only)

__VISA __ MC __ AmEx Card #_____Exp.Date_____

Signature _____ Day Phone _____

__Bill Me (U.S. institutional orders only. Purchase order required.)

Purchase order # _____
        Federal Tax ID13559302   **GST 89102 8052**

Name _____

Address _____

_____

Phone _____ E-mail _____

For more information about Jossey-Bass, visit our Web site at www.josseybass.com

SS110   Developing Social Justice Allies
         Robert D. Reason, Ellen M. Broido, Tracy L. Davis, Nancy J. Evans
         Social justice allies are individuals from dominant groups (for example,
         whites, heterosexuals, men) who work to end the oppression of target group
         members (people of color, homosexuals, women). Student affairs
         professionals have a history of philosophical commitment to social justice,
         and this volume strives to provide the theoretical foundation and practical
         strategies to encourage the development of social justice and civil rights
         allies among students and colleagues.
         ISBN: 0-7879-8077-3

SS109   Serving Native American Students
         Mary Jo Tippeconnic Fox, Shelly C. Lowe, George S. McClellan
         The increasing Native American enrollment on campuses nationwide is
         something to celebrate; however, the retention rate for Native American
         students is the lowest in higher education, a point of tremendous concern.
         This volume's authors—most of them Native American—address topics such
         as enrollment trends, campus experiences, cultural traditions, student
         services, ignorance about Indian country issues, expectations of tribal
         leaders and parents, and other challenges and opportunities encountered by
         Native students.
         ISBN: 0-7879-7971-6

SS108   Using Entertainment Media in Student Affairs Teaching and Practice
         Deanna S. Forney, Tony W. Cawthon
         Reaching all students may require going beyond traditional methods,
         especially in the out-of-classroom environments typical to student affairs.
         Using films, music, television shows, and popular books can help students
         learn. This volume—good for both practitioners and educators—shares
         effective approaches to using entertainment media to facilitate
         understanding of general student development, multiculturalism, sexual
         orientation, gender issues, leadership, counseling, and more.
         ISBN: 0-7879-7926-0

SS107   Developing Effective Programs and Services for College Men
         Gar E. Kellom
         This volume's aim is to better understand the challenges facing college men,
         particularly at-risk men. Topics include enrollment, retention, academic
         performance, women's college perspectives, men's studies perspectives,
         men's health issues, emotional development, and spirituality. Delivers
         recommendations and examples about programs and services that improve
         college men's learning experiences and race, class, and gender awareness.
         ISBN: 0-7879-7772-1

SS106   Serving the Millennial Generation
         Michael D. Coomes, Robert DeBard
         Focuses on the next enrollment boom, students born after 1981, known as
         the Millennial generation. Examines these students' attitudes, beliefs, and
         behaviors, and makes recommendations to student affairs practitioners for
         working with them. Discusses historical and cultural influences that shape
         generations, demographics, teaching and learning patterns of Millennials,
         and how student affairs can best educate and serve them.
         ISBN: 0-7879-7606-7

SS105   Addressing the Unique Needs of Latino American Students
         Anna M. Ortiz
         Explores the experiences of the fast-growing population of Latinos in higher
         education, and what these students need from student affairs. This volume
         examines the influence of the Latino family, socioeconomic levels, cultural
         barriers, and other factors to understand the challenges faced by Latinos.

Discusses administration, student groups, community colleges, support programs, cultural identity, Hispanic-Serving Institutions, and more.
ISBN: 0-7879-7479-X

SS104   **Meeting the Needs of African American Women**
Mary F. Howard-Hamilton
Identifies and explores the critical needs for African American women as students, faculty, and administrators. This volume introduces theoretical frameworks and practical applications for addressing challenges; discusses identity and spirituality; explores the importance of programming support in recruitment and retention; describes the benefits of mentoring; and provides illuminating case studies of black women's issues in higher education.
ISBN: 0-7879-7280-0

SS103   **Contemporary Financial Issues in Student Affairs**
John H. Schuh
This volume addresses the challenging financial situation facing higher education and offers creative solutions for student affairs staff. Topics include the differences between public and private institutions in funding student activities, how to demonstrate financial accountability to stakeholders, plus ways to address budget challenges in student unions, health centers, campus recreation, counseling centers, and student housing.
ISBN: 0-7879-7173-1

SS102   **Meeting the Special Needs of Adult Students**
Deborah Kilgore, Penny J. Rice
This volume examines the ways student services professionals can best help adult learners. Chapters highlight the specific challenges that adult enrollment brings to traditional four-year and postgraduate institutions, which are often focused on the traditional-aged student experience. Explaining that adult students are typically involved in campus life in different ways than younger students are, the volume provides student services professionals with good guidance on serving an ever-growing population.
ISBN: 0-7879-6991-5

SS101   **Planning and Achieving Successful Student Affairs Facilities Projects**
Jerry Price
Provides student affairs professionals with an examination of critical facilities issues by exploring the experiences of their colleagues. Illustrates that students' educational experiences are affected by residence halls, student unions, dining services, recreation and wellness centers, and campus grounds, and that student affairs professionals make valuable contributions to the success of campus facility projects. Covers planning, budgeting, collaboration, and communication through case studies and lessons learned.
ISBN: 0-7879-6847-1

SS100   **Student Affairs and External Relations**
Mary Beth Snyder
Building positive relations with external constituents is as important in student affairs work as it is in any other university or college division. This issue is a long-overdue resource of ideas, strategies, and information aimed at making student affairs leaders more effective in their interactions with important off-campus partners, supporters, and agencies. Chapter authors explore the current challenges facing the student services profession as well as the emerging opportunities worthy of student affairs interest.
ISBN: 0-7879-6342-9

**NEW DIRECTIONS FOR STUDENT SERVICES
IS NOW AVAILABLE ONLINE AT WILEY INTERSCIENCE**

What is Wiley InterScience?

Wiley InterScience is the dynamic online content service from John Wiley & Sons delivering the full text of over 300 leading scientific, technical, medical, and professional journals, plus major reference works, the acclaimed *Current Protocols* laboratory manuals, and even the full text of select Wiley print books online.

What are some special features of Wiley InterScience?

Wiley InterScience Alerts is a service that delivers table of contents via e-mail for any journal available on Wiley InterScience as soon as a new issue is published online.
Early View is Wiley's exclusive service presenting individual articles online as soon as they are ready, even before the release of the compiled print issue. These articles are complete, peer-reviewed, and citable.
CrossRef is the innovative multi-publisher reference linking system enabling readers to move seamlessly from a reference in a journal article to the cited publication, typically located on a different server and published by a different publisher.

How can I access Wiley InterScience?

Visit http://www.interscience.wiley.com

Guest Users can browse Wiley InterScience for unrestricted access to journal Tables of Contents and Article Abstracts, or use the powerful search engine.
Registered Users are provided with a *Personal Home Page* to store and manage customized alerts, searches, and links to favorite journals and articles. Additionally, Registered Users can view free Online Sample Issues and preview selected material from major reference works.
Licensed Customers are entitled to access full-text journal articles in PDF, with select journals also offering full-text HTML.

How do I become an Authorized User?

Authorized Users are individuals authorized by a paying Customer to have access to the journals in Wiley InterScience. For example, a university that subscribes to Wiley journals is considered to be the Customer. Faculty, staff and students authorized by the university to have access to those journals in Wiley InterScience are Authorized Users. Users should contact their Library for information on which Wiley journals they have access to in Wiley InterScience.

ASK YOUR INSTITUTION ABOUT WILEY INTERSCIENCE TODAY!

United States Postal Service

Statement of Ownership, Management, and Circulation

1. Publication Title	2. Publication Number	3. Filing Date
New Directions For Student Services	0 1 6 4 _ 7 9 7 0	10/1/06

4. Issue Frequency	5. Number of Issues Published Annually	6. Annual Subscription Price
Quarterly	4	$195.00

7. Complete Mailing Address of Known Office of Publication (Not printer) (Street, city, county, state, and ZIP+4)	Contact Person
Wiley Subscription Services, Inc. at Jossey-Bass, 989 Market Street, San Francisco, CA 94103	Joe Schuman Telephone (415) 782-3232

8. Complete Mailing Address of Headquarters or General Business Office of Publisher (Not printer)

Wiley Subscription Services, Inc. 111 River Street, Hoboken, NJ 07030

9. Full Names and Complete Mailing Addresses of Publisher, Editor, and Managing Editor (Do not leave blank)

Publisher (Name and complete mailing address)

Wiley Subscription Services, Inc., A Wiley Company at San Francisco, 989 Market Street, San Francisco, CA 94103-1741

Editor (Name and complete mailing address)

John H. Schuh, N243 Lagomarcino Hall, Iowa State University, Ames, IA 50011

Managing Editor (Name and complete mailing address)

None

10. Owner (Do not leave blank. If the publication is owned by a corporation, give the name and address of the corporation immediately followed by the names and addresses of all stockholders owning or holding 1 percent or more of the total amount of stock. If not owned by a corporation, give the names and addresses of the individual owners. If owned by a partnership or other unincorporated firm, give its name and address as well as those of each individual owner. If the publication is published by a nonprofit organization, give its name and address.)

Full Name	Complete Mailing Address
Wiley Subscription Services, Inc.	111 River Street, Hoboken, NJ 07030
(see attached list)	

11. Known Bondholders, Mortgagees, and Other Security Holders Owning or Holding 1 Percent or More of Total Amount of Bonds, Mortgages, or Other Securities. If none, check box ———————— ▶ ☑ None

Full Name	Complete Mailing Address
None	None

12. Tax Status (For completion by nonprofit organizations authorized to mail at nonprofit rates) (Check one)
The purpose, function, and nonprofit status of this organization and the exempt status for federal income tax purposes:
☐ Has Not Changed During Preceding 12 Months
☐ Has Changed During Preceding 12 Months (Publisher must submit explanation of change with this statement)

13. Publication Title New Directions For Student Services	14. Issue Date for Circulation Data Below Summer 2006

15. Extent and Nature of Circulation			Average No. Copies Each Issue During Preceding 12 Months	No. Copies of Single Issue Published Nearest to Filing Date
a. Total Number of Copies (Net press run)			1555	1683
b. Paid and/or Requested Circulation	(1)	Paid/Requested Outside-County Mail Subscriptions Stated on Form 3541. (Include advertiser's proof and exchange copies)	474	468
	(2)	Paid In-County Subscriptions Stated on Form 3541 (Include advertiser's proof and exchange copies)	0	0
	(3)	Sales Through Dealers and Carriers, Street Vendors, Counter Sales, and Other Non-USPS Paid Distribution	0	0
	(4)	Other Classes Mailed Through the USPS	0	0
c. Total Paid and/or Requested Circulation [Sum of 15b. (1), (2),(3),and (4)]		▶	474	468
d. Free Distribution by Mail (Samples, complimentary, and other free)	(1)	Outside-County as Stated on Form 3541	0	0
	(2)	In-County as Stated on Form 3541	0	0
	(3)	Other Classes Mailed Through the USPS	0	0
e. Free Distribution Outside the Mail (Carriers or other means)			89	87
f. Total Free Distribution (Sum of 15d. and 15e.)		▶	89	87
g. Total Distribution (Sum of 15c. and 15f)		▶	563	555
h. Copies not Distributed			992	1128
i. Total (Sum of 15g. and h.)		▶	1555	1683
j. Percent Paid and/or Requested Circulation (15c. divided by 15g. times 100)			84%	84%

16. Publication of Statement of Ownership
☑ Publication required. Will be printed in the Winter 2006 issue of this publication. ☐ Publication not required.

17. Signature and Title of Editor, Publisher, Business Manager, or Owner	Date
Susan E. Lewis, VP & Publisher - Periodicals	10/01/06

I certify that all information furnished on this form is true and complete. I understand that anyone who furnishes false or misleading information on this form or who omits material or information requested on the form may be subject to criminal sanctions (including fines and imprisonment) and/or civil sanctions (including civil penalties).